D1084585

The Tangled Fire of William Faulkner

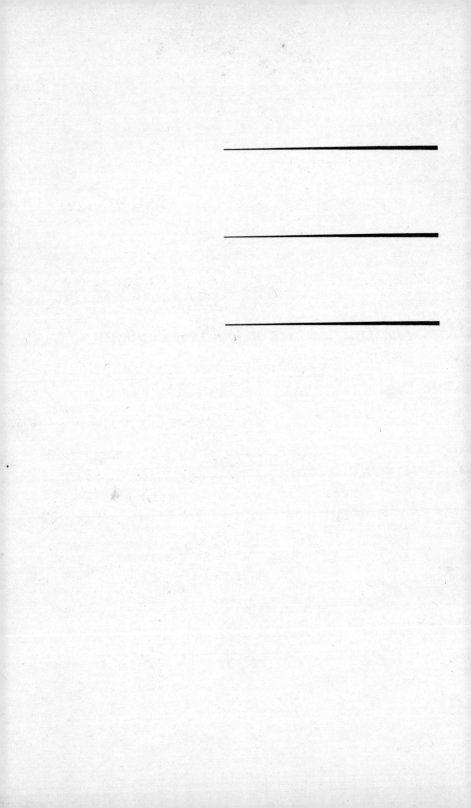

The TANGLED FIRE *of* WILLIAM FAULKNER

BY WILLIAM VAN O'CONNOR

GORDIAN PRESS, INC.
NEW YORK
1968

Originally Published 1954
Reprinted 1968

813.52
F26320

Library of Congress Catalog #68-22386

© Copyright 1954 by The
University of Minnesota

Published by
GORDIAN PRESS INC.

By arrangement with the University of Minnesota

for Van and Lee

I want to perform something bold and tragical and austere he repeated, shaping the soundless words in the pattering silence *me on a buckskin pony with eyes like blue electricity and a mane like tangled fire, galloping up the hill and right off into the high heaven of the world . . .*

"CARCASSONNE"

Preface

THE purpose of this book is to offer a coherent interpretation of Faulkner's fiction. It introduces as much biographical information as seems to me useful in accounting for the man in relation to his fiction and the man in relation to his region. Primarily, however, this is a critical study. Therefore, some of the biographical information I have collected, which is of interest but not especially relevant to an interpretation of Faulkner's fiction, I have included only in the notes, for the most part, at the back of the book.

At this point in the history of Faulkner criticism, it will seem to some readers necessary to justify another book on Faulkner. The justification, as I see it, is best made in negative terms, in mentioning what strike me as limitations in the criticism that centers attention on the "Southern Myth." This criticism was begun by George Marion O'Donnell, then extended and modified by Malcolm Cowley and Robert Penn Warren. Its influence, which has been remarkable and pervasive, is accounted for by the fact that the overall view does have a degree of relevancy far greater than that of almost any of the criticism which preceded it; by and large, the early Faulkner criticism was shockingly wrong-headed. And that I may not seem too ungracious I want to add that the present study, while in disagreement at many points, is also greatly indebted to commentaries on Faulkner's "legend of the South," either by these three critics or others who, similarly, are indebted to them.

The Tangled Fire of William Faulkner

In general this criticism sees Faulkner glorifying a Past that was lived in gloriously by members of the planter-aristocracy, whose way of life managed to bathe even the nonslaveholding classes in virtue. And it sees him opposing Modernism, amoral, self-interested, sensation-seeking, to this Past. Sometimes the honorific word is Tradition, which connotes honor, integrity, and *noblesse oblige*. But let us use Mr. Warren's summary of the Cowley thesis (which Mr. Warren says is built upon the O'Donnell thesis):

The South was settled by Sartorises (aristocrats) and Sutpens (nameless, ambitious men) who, seizing the land from the Indians, were determined to found an enduring and stable order. But despite their strength and integrity their project was, to use Faulkner's word, "accursed" by slavery, which, with the Civil War as instrument, frustrated their design. Their attempt to rebuild according to the old plan and old values was defeated by a combination of forces — the carpetbaggers and Snopeses ("a new exploiting class descended from the landless whites"). Most of the descendants of the old order are in various ways incompetent: They are prevented by their code from competing with the codeless Snopeses, they cling to the letter and forget the spirit of their tradition, they lose contact with the realities of the present and escape into a dream world of alcohol or rhetoric or gentility or madness, they fall in love with defeat or death, they lose nerve and become cowards, or they, like the last Jason in *The Sound and the Fury*, adopt Snopesism and become worse than any Snopes. Figures like Popeye (eyes like "rubber knobs," a creature having "that vicious depthless quality of stamped tin," the man "who made money and had nothing he could do with it, spend it for, since he knew that alcohol would kill him like poison, who had no friends and had never known a woman") are in their dehumanized quality symbols of modernism, for the society of finance capitalism. . . .

Mr. Warren, while observing the usefulness of this "history," says there is danger in following it too rigorously. There is indeed, for in some ways it is quite false: No Faulkner novel treats the ante-bellum South more than tangentially, and no novel shows either the Sartorises or Sutpens attempting to set up a moral, intellectual, or social order. Sutpen, who is the only man struggling to build, is trying to establish himself financially and to found a family — he accepts and is defeated by the mores, but he has no notion that he is building for anyone other than himself. None of the McCaslin forebears, seen retrospectively in *Go Down Moses*, is building the Old Order ("strength and integrity"); Uncle Bud and Uncle Buck, who refuse to have anything to do with slavery, retreat from the society.

Secondly, there are no significant carpetbaggers (the Burdens certainly are not carpetbaggers) among Faulkner's characters, and the Snopeses are in no sense typical of the descendants from the landless whites. Those among the Snopeses who are exploiters (not all of them are) do not develop their talent until they are in the twentieth-century world. And the landless whites, or "rednecks," and their descendants have provided Faulkner with some of his most intensely moral and admirable characters. Again, with the stunt fliers of *Pylon* as evidence, it is clear that Faulkner has a margin of admiration for some of the products of Modernism, though it is true that there are also aspects of the modern world which he despises. The evil in *Sanctuary* is of two sorts: a world in decay, reminiscent of nineteenth-century weltschmerz literature, and a world of mechanism.

Briefly, neither the Sartoris-Snopes formula nor the Traditional Past vs. an Amoral Present formula really works.

Faulkner did not begin his career with a schematized notion of southern history. His views are not all of a piece. Sometimes, as for example in *Light in August*, he is harshly critical of his region, and sometimes, as in *Intruder in the Dust*, he defends it. In *Sartoris* he defends, without probing, the protagonist's preoccupation with bravery, and the gallant gesture, but in *The Unvanquished*, as chapter succeeds chapter, we watch him becoming very quizzical about the virtues of the Old Order, with bravery becoming headlong heroics and honor becoming not personal dignity but a rationalization of a lust for murder. And there are of course books — *Soldiers' Pay, Mosquitoes, The Wild Palms, Pylon* — and a number of short stories which have their settings elsewhere than in northern Mississippi.

There is, I believe, a center in Faulkner that is constant, a faith in man as a being capable of selflessness, endurance, love, and honor. These virtues transcend class and are to be found in different places and at different periods. Opportunism and extreme self-righteousness, which he appears to despise almost equally, are the counterparts of the virtues; if they seem to be more common in the present than in the past, certainly they are not absent from the past, and it is possible that the righteousness that gives rise to persecution was even more common in the past.

A final word: I believe that Faulkner, although a greater writer, is a very uneven one, and in discussing those stories that seem to me to exhibit weaknesses, sometimes serious weaknesses, I have not hesitated to be adversely critical. Ultimately a writer's reputation stands not on what he failed to achieve, but on what he achieved.

W. V. O'C.

Minneapolis, Minnesota
August 1953

Acknowledgments

SECTIONS from this book, or at least ideas developed in it in somewhat similar form, have appeared in the following magazines: *Sewanee Review, Hopkins Review, Northern Review, Western Humanities Review, Southwest Review, Faulkner Studies,* and *Accent.* To the editors of these publications I am grateful for the opportunity to publish in their pages and for permission to use the material here. I have also talked and corresponded with a number of friends and associates of Faulkner and want to thank them for the information which they gave me.

Table of Contents

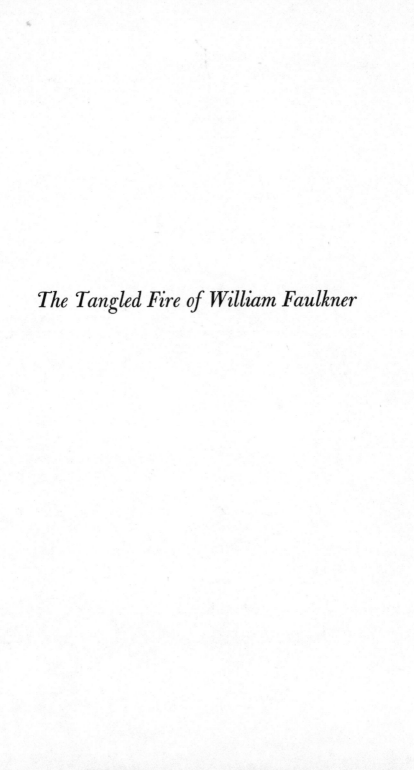

The Tangled Fire of William Faulkner

The Sartorises of Jefferson

Murray falkner and Maud Butler Falkner* had four children, William, Murray, John, and Dean, there being about seven years between William, the eldest, and Dean, the youngest. Some time ago, when asked about the childhood, in Oxford, Mississippi, of her author son, Maud Falkner said, "Bill was full of life and pep and played with the boys on his street in a perfectly normal way." He did have, she said, a greater than usual curiosity and imagination. Enlisting the help of his brothers, especially John, he built mechanical toys and experimented with chemicals. An investigation into the mysterious properties of the chemicals then used in flashlight photography temporarily cost John both eyebrows. Another experiment cost twelve Wyandotte hens their lives. Bill and his brother had wanted to find out what the effects would be of dipping the hens into a can of paint. When the paint dried the hens couldn't lift their wings. "They died," Mrs. Falkner said, "with their boots on, sitting up."

She also called attention to Bill's interest in telling stories. He sometimes made up fairy and Indian stories to entertain his brothers while they did the chores, including his share of them. At

* A printer's error in setting up the title page of *The Marble Faun* seems responsible for the *u* in Faulkner. *Who's Who* still lists him as William Falkner.

twelve, he hand-printed a penny-a-copy newspaper which chronicled the affairs of the Falkner block on South Street. Bill was always, his mother said, interested in unusual words which he used accurately and rarely forgot.[1]

Some of the townspeople remember him as a recalcitrant student interested in English and little else. Miss Ella Wright, a cousin of Stark Young and the aunt-in-law of Dr. Pursur, the Baptist minister, remembers William as a quiet, dark-eyed child who did little to distinguish himself among his classmates. Mrs. Calvin Brown, widow of the former head of the Romance languages department at the state university in Oxford, recalls one evening when "Billy came to Mr. Brown and asked him whether studying mathematics would help him to think more clearly. They sat out on the gallery all evening discussing it."

In high school Bill was quarterback on the football team. Playing against Oxford's bitter rival, the high school at Holly Springs, he had his nose broken. In the tenth grade, after irregular attendance for two or three years, he left school and Grandfather Falkner gave him a place in the bank. Details of his brief career there have to be inferred as best one can from Faulkner's own elliptical account: "Quit school and went to work in Grandfather's bank. Learned the medicinal value of his liquor. Grandfather thought it was the janitor. Hard on the janitor. . . ."

It is necessary to look into the Falkner family history and into the history of Oxford, because the family becomes the Sartoris clan and Oxford becomes the Jefferson of Faulkner's fiction. The branch of the Falkner family from which William derives moved to Tennessee out of the Carolinas.[2] William C. Falkner, great-grandfather of the author, was born in Knox County, Tennessee, on July 6, 1825. His parents moved on from Tennessee to Saint Genevieve, Missouri, where the father died, leaving several young children. William C., the eldest, with the responsibility of helping to support the family, set out for Ripley, Mississippi, to live with an uncle, John W. Thompson. He walked the several hundred miles to Ripley — only to find upon his arrival that his uncle, a school-

4

teacher, was in jail at Pontotoc, charged with murder. The boy walked on to Pontotoc, where, exhausted and disheartened, he sat on the steps of an inn and wept. A little girl, taking pity on him, told the landlord of Anderson's tavern, who took the boy in, fed him, and sent him back to Ripley.

Eventually the uncle was freed from the murder charge. During his stay in jail he had given himself earnestly to studying law and upon his release opened a law practice in Ripley. William C. studied law in his uncle's office and practiced it all his life except for a period spent fighting in the Mexican War (he was a first lieutenant) and his years in the Civil War.

When the Civil War broke out, William C. helped to organize the Second Mississippi Regiment, and was elected its colonel. He was at Harpers Ferry, took a significant part in the first battle of Manassas, and fought in several hard engagements. General Joseph E. Johnson wrote a strong letter of commendation for him to the War Department in April 1862. The troops in his regiment, however, chose a new commander, a Colonel Stone, to replace him. According to his great-grandson, William C. was replaced because his discipline was too severe. Upon his return to Mississippi he organized the First Mississippi Partisan Rangers, which became the Seventh Mississippi Cavalry, serving under General Chalmers and General Bedford Forrest.

At the War's end, William C. conceived the notion of running a line of railroad from Pontotoc to a point just inside the Tennessee line, at Middleton, where it would intersect the Memphis and Charleston railroad. It was only a narrow-gauge line, but because of William C.'s hopes for it he called it the "Gulf, Ship Island, Ripley and Kentucky Railroad." Later it became the Gulf, Mobile and Ohio Railroad.

William C. was also a successful author. He wrote *The Little Brick Church, Rapid Ramblings in Europe*, and *The White Rose of Memphis*, the latter selling 160,000 copies by 1909, the date of the thirty-fifth edition.

William C.'s first wife died within a year or two of their marriage, leaving one son, named John W. Thompson Falkner; his second marriage was to Miss Elizabeth Vance, who had been the little girl who befriended him upon his arrival in Pontotoc!

As a young man, in 1849, William C. had resisted an attack by Robert Hindman, finally being forced, in self-defense, to stab him. In the ensuing trial he was acquitted of murder. Leaving the courtroom after the acquittal, William C. was attacked by Thomas Hindman and a man named Morris. In that fight Morris was killed. Again William C. was acquitted. The Hindmans and William C. had served together in the Mexican War, but no one seems to know very clearly what the reason was for their violent attempts on his life. Shortly after the second trial Thomas Hindman tried but failed to shoot him, and a duel was arranged. Before the duel could be fought, William C. convinced responsible people that he knew of no reason for the duel and it was prevented, with Hindman leaving Mississippi.

The circumstances of William C.'s death, according to the Jackson, Mississippi, *Clarion-Ledger*, November 14, 1889, were these:

A terrible tragedy was enacted at Ripley on Tuesday afternoon of last week — the widely and well-known Col. W. C. Falkner being the victim. Various and conflicting accounts have been published. A dispatch to the *Appeal* says:

"At the time of the occurrence Col. Falkner was standing on the public square in Ripley, talking to his friend Thomas Rucker, about sawing some timber. Mr. J. H. Thurmond approached Falkner and without exchanging a word pulled out a pistol and pointed it at Col. Falkner who exclaimed, 'What do you mean, Dick? Don't shoot!' but Thurmond fired and Falkner fell.

"After Dr. Carter, his son-in-law, wiped the blood from his face while he was still sitting on the pavement, he (Falkner) turned to Thurmond, who was near him, and said: 'Dick, what did you do it for?' J. L. Walker, Elisha Bryant, Tom Rucker and John Smith were all present and saw what occurred. . . . Col. Falkner died at 11 o'clock."

Thurmond was tried for murder and acquitted in a highly sensational trial. He then moved to North Carolina and became a leading figure in the textile industry. The Falkner family has this interpretation of the murder: In financing the railroad, William C. was associated with Thurmond, a leading businessman in Ripley.

The Sartorises of Jefferson

At a point when William C.'s fortunes seemed to be bad, Thurmond came forward with the proposition that for the sum of $19,000 either he or his partner would withdraw. Having foreseen the move, William C. had borrowed the money to buy Thurmond out, and this made Thurmond an enemy. Thurmond's hatred was increased when, years later in 1889, Falkner won a seat in the state legislature, defeating Thurmond for it. On election day, according to the family story, William C. verified the results, and then, knowing Thurmond intended to kill him but being determined not to fight any more duels or kill any more men, he walked across to Thurmond's office and offered no defense when Thurmond came to the door and shot him.

It is clear enough that William C. was a legendary figure in the area. A life-sized monument of him is in the Ripley cemetery, facing his railroad.

William C.'s son, J. W. T. Falkner, was also a lawyer, and he practiced for a time at Ripley. Later, in Oxford, he was Assistant United States Attorney for the Northern District of Mississippi. He represented the Illinois Central Railroad, and he was the president of the First National Bank of Oxford. Undoubtedly he is the basis for Banker Sartoris who appears frequently in the life of Jefferson. Grandfather Falkner was also an associate of Senator James Kemble Vardaman, the political leader of the "rednecks" or tenant farmers.[3] (Appropriately, one of the Bundren children, the "redneck" family of *As I Lay Dying*, is named Vardaman.) In law practice he had as partner Lee M. Russell, later governor of Mississippi. There is a story still told in Oxford that Governor Russell once came to pay an evening call but that Banker Falkner, opening the door and seeing who it was, said, "Mistah Russell, our relationship is purely bus'ness and political, not social!" and closed the door on him. He is remembered as a testy old man, usually dressed in immaculate white, very bald and very deaf.

Grandfather Falkner had married Miss Sallie Murray of Ripley. They had three children: Murray C. Falkner, father of William; Mrs. Holland Falkner Williams of Oxford; and J. W. T. Falkner, Jr., a leading Oxford lawyer, a circuit judge, a trustee of the

7

university, and a successful political figure. The Murray family, like the Falkners, were noted for their frankness, and Faulkner's grandmother was especially famous for giving, with or without request, the "quiveringly naked truth." It was she who said of her grandson that as a child he was an angel for three weeks and a devil the fourth.

Murray C. Falkner as a young man served as a railroad conductor, as an auditor, and still later as a depot agent in New Albany, the seat of Union County, Mississippi. It was there, in 1897, that William was born. In 1902 Murray Falkner moved his family to Oxford, where he successively ran a livery stable and a hardware store. For some years before his retirement in 1931, he was business manager for the University of Mississippi. Maud Butler, his wife, had as a girl attended the Industrial Institute and College (later Mississippi State College for Women) and she had shown some talent for drawing and painting. According to some of the older residents of Oxford, however, it was her mother who had the more significant talent, and it is to this grandmother, they insist, that William owes his gifts as an artist. Maud Butler Falkner still resides in Oxford — and she is quite willing to talk about her son William's achievements.

Faulkner's family appear in his works as the Sartorises.* Two novels, *Sartoris* and *The Unvanquished*, are devoted to them. The murder of William C. Falkner takes this form in *Sartoris*:

It showed on John Sartoris' brow, the dark shadow of fatality and doom, that night when he sat beneath the candles in the dining room and turned a wineglass in his fingers while he talked to his son. The railroad was finished, and that day he had been elected to the state legislature after a hard and bitter fight, and doom lay on his brow, and weariness.

"And so," he said, "Redlaw will kill me tomorrow, for I shall be unarmed. I'm tired of killing men. . . . Pass the wine, Bayard. . . ."

And the next day he was dead.

* According to Faulkner's friend Phil Stone, who suggested the use of the name, the accent falls on the first syllable: Sar'to·ris.

The Sartorises of Jefferson

That the family is (or once was) romantic in Faulkner's eyes is suggested by this passage near the end of *Sartoris*: "For there is death in the sound of it [the name Sartoris] and a glamorous fatality, like silver pennons downrushing at sunset, or a dying fall of horns along the road to Roncevaux." The youthful Faulkner himself bears more than a slight resemblance to young Bayard, protagonist of *Sartoris*, the World War I aviator returned to Jefferson.

Commentators on the Jefferson saga sometimes imply that Faulkner's antecedents were wealthy planters. This obviously is not true. Colonel William C. Falkner was one of the "new men," and J. W. T. Falkner, whatever his desires or private allegiances may have been, was involved with the political fortunes of the small tenant farmers, the very people who had in effect been disenfranchised during the old order. In *Sartoris* one of the characters says that a Flem Snopes would not have been allowed in the Confederate Army: "General Johnson or General Forrest wouldn't have took a Snopes into his army at all." But Flem Snopes *is* vice-president in Bayard Sartoris' bank because locally he is politically useful. Faulkner has also used the Compson family, as in *The Sound and the Fury* and *Absalom! Absalom!*, to dramatize the conflict between the concepts of honor of the aristocratic tradition and the money-grubbing new order he calls Snopesism. In *Sanctuary* we see poor Horace Benbow almost sick with self-contempt when he is forced to make a deal with Clarence Snopes, Mississippi state senator.

In the opening pages of *The Hamlet*, the novel primarily devoted to the Snopes saga, Will Varner — "a milder mannered man never bled a mule or stuffed a ballot box" — is sitting in front of a decayed manor house, against a "background of fallen baronial splendor":

The people (those who saw him sitting there and those who were told about it) all believed that he sat there planning his next mortgage foreclosure in private, since it was only to an itinerant sewing-machine agent named Ratliff — a man less than half his age — that he ever gave a reason: "I like to sit here. I'm trying to

9

find out what it must have felt like to be the fool that would need all this" — he did not move, he did not so much as indicate with his head the rise of old brick and tangled walks topped by the columned ruin behind him — "just to eat and sleep in." Then he said — and he gave Ratliff no further clue to which might have been the truth — "For a while it looked like I was going to get shut of it, get it cleared up. But by God folks have got so lazy they won't even climb a ladder to pull off the rest of the boards. It looks like they will go into the woods and even chop up a tree before they will reach above eyelevel for a scantling of pine kindling. But after all, I reckon I'll just keep what there is left of it, just to remind me of my one mistake. This is the only thing I ever bought in my life I couldn't sell to nobody."

For at least two generations after the War, the upper social stratum continued to control the political life of northern Mississippi. The former slave owners and members of their class, many of whom had been officers in the War, continued to exert an influence over the mass of small landholding tenants, most of whom had very little education. They ran their own Democratic party convention and nominated their own candidates. But with the coming of the primary election system, there began, especially through the efforts of James Kemble Vardaman, "The Great White Chief," the day of the "redneck." This meant that the people themselves did the nominating and the tenant farmer's vote counted as much as that of a descendant of the plantation owner. Unscrupulous office seekers were free to play upon the desires of country people who had not yet learned to employ the franchise intelligently and who undoubtedly had grievances against the group who had previously kept them from having a voice in their government. Eventually, with the coming of the automobile and the easier spread of information, these abuses became less flagrant. The "rise of the redneck" is significant in the life of William Faulkner because, as Phil Stone, Faulkner's friend, puts it, he "was born before the movement got under way and passed his life until manhood in the very middle of it, his grandfather and his only uncle [J. W. T. Falkner, Jr.] being leaders in the following of Vardaman," his agents in Lafayette County. Into *The Hamlet*

William Faulkner has put some of his grimmest humor. It is not beyond imagining that tensions within his own family furnished him with some of it.

It is quite true, however, that the Sartorises are elevated into glamorous legend. For example, there is this recommendation in *The Unvanquished* by Uncle Buck, who is one of Faulkner's voices of decency and wisdom:

"Fools, I say!" he shouted. "I don't care if some of you folks here do still claim kin with men that elected him colonel and followed him and Stonewall Jackson right up to spitting distance of Washington without hardly losing a man, and then next year turned around and voted him down to major and elected in his stead a damn feller that never even knowed which end of a gun done the shooting until John Sartoris showed him." He quit shouting just as easy as he started but the shouting was right there, waiting to start again as soon as he found something else to shout about. "I won't say God take care of you and your grandma on the road, boy, because by Godfrey you don't need God's nor nobody else's help; all you got to say is 'I'm John Sartoris' boy; rabbits, hunt the canebrake' and then watch the blue-bellied sons of bitches fly."

The Unvanquished for most of its length develops a dashing, glamorous view of Colonel Sartoris and of Drusilla, a heroine worthy of riding with a troop of beautiful Amazons in a medieval or Renaissance romance. But this earlier part of the book is related by the boy Bayard. Suddenly, in the final section, "Odor of Verbena," when Bayard is adult, much of what he had taken for granted is repudiated: the right to kill for one's dignity or in the service of the old order, for instance, and the pursuit of disaster for the sheer romance of it. Bayard refuses to continue the feuding with Redlaw, and he as narrator gives this account of the scene in which he apprises his father's associates and friends that the retribution, whatever it is to be, is in his, not their, hands:

Then I saw Drusilla standing at the top of the front steps, in the light from the open door and the windows like a theater scene, in the yellow ball gown and even from here I believed that I could smell the verbena in her hair, standing there motionless yet emanating something louder than the two shots must have been —

11

something voracious too and passionate. Then, although I had dismounted and someone had taken the mare, I seemed to be still in the saddle and to watch myself enter that scene which she has postulated like another actor while in the background for chorus Wyatt and the others stood with the unctuous formality which the Southern man shows in the presence of death — that Roman holiday engendered by mist-born Protestantism grafted onto this land of violent sun, of violent alteration from snow to heat-stroke which has produced a race impervious to both.

There is, obviously, a good deal of irony and disbelief in Bayard. He approves, as the rest of the story makes clear, the sense of dignity, the concept of honor, and the need for courage, but he is disapproving of the ease with which the code invited excesses, staginess, and impersonality.

The land on which Oxford stands was ceded to the government by the Chickasaws in 1832, and according to the marker in front of the courthouse, the town was chartered in 1837.[4] The University of Mississippi opened there in 1848. No major Civil War battle was fought in or near Oxford, but there were several skirmishes in the neighborhood and several companies were raised in Lafayette County, mostly from the university. In the final years of the War, Oxford was entered frequently by northern troops. Grant, who refers briefly to Oxford in his *Memoirs*, stopped there in a push on Vicksburg, and on the pane of the front door of the house in which Phil Stone lived Faulkner often read: "U. S. Grant, 1862." A local legend has it that Grant called North Lamar Street the loveliest street he had ever seen. And Celia Cook, the girl who married General Nathan Bedford Forrest, lived in Oxford.

In "Ambuscade," the opening section of *The Unvanquished*, Faulkner's young narrator tells how the war came, first by word of mouth and later in action, to Oxford, or, as the town exists in his fiction, to Jefferson:

Ringo and I squatted on either side of the hearth, beneath the mantel above which the captured musket which he had brought home from Virginia two years ago rested on two pegs, loaded and oiled for service. Then we listened. We heard: the names — Forrest and Morgan and Barksdale and Van Dorn; the words like Gap and Run which we didn't have in Mississippi even though we did own Barksdale, and Van Dorn until somebody's husband killed him, and one day General Forrest rode down South Street in Oxford where there watched him through a windowpane a young girl who scratched her name on it with a diamond ring: Celia Cook.

After the battle of Shiloh a hospital was set up at the university and was furnished with beds, mattresses, and linens by the townspeople. The surgeon in charge of the hospital was Thomas Dudley Isom, who as a young man of eighteen, in 1835, had opened the first trading store on the site that shortly was to be Oxford and then left to complete his education. (A minor character named Isom appears in *Sartoris* and in *Sanctuary*.) Fifteen thousand soldiers were attended to at the hospital. In August 1864 Federal troops under General A. J. Smith burned all but one of the main business structures in the town. Naturally the echoes of such events are frequent in Faulkner's stories, perhaps the most conspicuously haunted character being Gail Hightower, of *Light in August*, who lives with the vision of his grandfather's being shot from the saddle during a raid in Jefferson. In "The Jail," the long documentary account of Jefferson in *Requiem for a Nun*, Faulkner has described the fire thus:

That night the town was occupied by Federal troops; two nights later, it was on fire (the Square, the stores and shops and the professional offices), gutted (the courthouse too), the blackened jagged topless jumbles of brick wall enclosing like a ruined jaw the blackened shell of the courthouse between its two rows of topless columns, which (the columns) were only blackened and stained, being tougher than fire: but not the jail, it escaped, untouched, insulated by fire or perhaps cauterised by fire from fury and turmoil, the long roar of the rushing omnivorous rock fading on to the east with the fading uproar of battle; and so in effect it was a whole year in advance of Appomattox. . . .

Oxford, the county seat, now has a population of about four thousand; it is on Mississippi state highways Number 6, 7, and 30; and it is on the Illinois Central Railroad that runs from Granada, Mississippi, to Fulton, Kentucky. Once when William Faulk-

13

ner was in New York, to help ballyhoo *Sanctuary,* he wrote a friend back home that he "felt sorry for all these millions of people here because they don't live in Oxford." According to Phil Stone, one has to understand the region around Oxford before one can understand Faulkner, and Stone has described it as it impresses him, a native and life-long resident:

From any part of Oxford it is only a little walk to numerous places where one can find the unspoiled golden peace of legendary days and where the sound of mankind's so-called progress comes only dreamlike and afar. . . . There are rows on serried rows of far hills, blue and purple and lavender and lilac in the sun, hills upon which you can look day after day and year after year and never find light and shadow and color exactly the same. . . . Here, out of the contemporary mad rush, we have time and quiet to think and savor the taste of things. . . . Here on frosty nights of fall we have only to listen to hear, faint and afar, the bay of the hunting hound, as in *Sartoris* — "mournful and valiant and a little sad." [5]

To the long-time resident the region around Oxford undoubtedly has this loveliness. But it is also, and this strikes the outlander harshly and immediately, a terribly abused land; erosion, caused by excessive cutting of timber and failure to rotate crops, has left great gaps or gulches in the red clay and washed away much of the top soil. The shacks, Negro and white alike, that line the roads of northern Mississippi bespeak hardship and poverty. Although an Oxford or a Holly Springs seems to have adapted successfully enough to the slowly changing order, other towns emit an odor of decay. A few are ghosts. In this part of the state almost nothing remains (and because of its late settlement there never was much) of the old feudal magnificence. Now it is almost exclusively a country of shifting tenant farmers, black and white. There is little or no industrialization in or around Oxford.

Oxford has furnished Faulkner with many impressions, although not necessarily those another writer would take, and he has used them for his own purposes. One of his frequent themes is the relationship of the past to the present, and in Oxford, as in many southern towns, one has a sense of the past through old houses and public buildings as well as through the presence of elderly people who by desire as well as necessity have kept the past alive. Stories of the Civil War live more vividly in their memories than they do in the memories of their northern contemporaries. Little touched by recent immigration, Oxford has many families with a detailed knowledge of and reverence for their genealogy. But the South is also undergoing a leveling process, the consequences of mass communication and industrialism, and in Oxford today the movies, the drugstores, the houses are pretty much what they are in other American communities. Faulkner's own white-pillared, two-story house, set far back among cedar trees, is well over a hundred years old, one of the oldest houses in town, but most of the other houses on the street are simple little bungalows of the sort one sees in Indiana, Iowa, or Pennsylvania. There are also the slowly disappearing unpainted high-roofed cottages, such as the one described in "Spotted Horses," with a hall running the length of the house and opening into rooms on both sides.

In Oxford, Faulkner has lived with physical evidences of an older world and been the inheritor of some of its pieties. But he has worked hard to quicken what he found at hand, interpreting and transmuting it imaginatively. A man with little sense of charity who worked in the Oxford bank became the germ of Flem Snopes, the spirit of personal aggrandizement and meanness. Faulkner's friend Stone became the basis for Horace Benbow and Gavin Stevens. Stone's father became Major de Spain. The Stone hunting lodge became a symbolic tie with the primeval wilderness. And so on. Faulkner says he has written as much as he has of his home country because that is what he knows best.[6] And it is true that except for brief periods, his life, like that of his family before him, has been involved in the life of Lafayette and neighboring counties. But his life away from home, especially in his earlier years, was probably crucial in his development as a writer.

Period of Apprenticeship

FAULKNER'S FIRST PUBLISHED POEM was
"L'Apres Midi d'un Faune":

> I follow through the singing trees
> Her streaming clouded hair and face
> And lascivious dreaming knees
> Like gleaming water from some place
> Of sleeping streams, or autumn leaves
> Slow shed through still, love-wearied air . . .
>
> I have a nameless wish to go
> To some far silent midnight noon
> Where lonely streams whisper and flow
> And sigh on sands blanched by the moon,
> And blond-limbed dancers whirling past,
> The senile worn moon staring through
> The sighing trees, until at last,
> Their hair is powdered bright with dew.
> And their sad slow limbs and brows
> Are petals drifting on the breeze
> Shed from the fingers of the boughs;
> Then suddenly on all of these,
> A sound like some great deep bell stroke
> Falls, and they dance, unclad and cold —

NOTE: This chapter is reprinted, with modifications, from the original version in *Southwest Review*, vol. 38, no. 1 (Winter 1953), by permission of the editor.

Period of Apprenticeship

It was the earth's great heart that broke
For springs before the world grew old.[1]

Obviously the shimmer of the 1890s is in this poem — of Yeats
saying "all art is dream," of O'Shaughnessy envisioning the poet
as a world-forsaker under the pale and gleaming moon, or of
Symons finding esthetic delight in the mysterious pallor of skin
in the starlight.

The *fin de siècle* writers, experts in expressing a wan disillusion-
ment, were a strong influence on the young writers that left college
in 1917 for service overseas, a generation that was to write its share
of the literature of despair in the 1920s. In *Exile's Return* Malcolm
Cowley described the Harvard of John Dos Passos, E. E. Cum-
mings, and himself as "an after-image of Oxford in the 1890s."
Youthful writers trying to look like "prematurely decayed poets"
read Swinburne, Walter Pater, Ernest Dowson, Lionel Johnson,
and Oscar Wilde, and studied the art of Aubrey Beardsley. They
learned that one could be dissipated and yet faithful after one's
fashion, that life should be lived as ritual, and that the Church
was ancient wisdom, not unmixed with voluptuousness. At Prince-
ton John Peale Bishop and F. Scott Fitzgerald were translating
Verlaine, who with Swinburne would help set the tone of *This
Side of Paradise* (1919). Fitzgerald's Amory Blaine took his place
in the tradition of the young esthete as protagonist, like Pater's
Marius, Huysman's Esseintes, and Wilde's Dorian Gray, all of
whom were shown in retreat from a crass, machine-made civilization. Another part of the tradition was the ripeness and decay and
sin of Baudelaire, the subtle evocations of Mallarmé, and the
almost brittle ironies of Laforgue. In other words, Fitzgerald —
who in the politics-ridden 1930s would say, "Back to Mallarmé!"
— was writing in the tradition which had been analyzed by Arthur
Symons in *The Symbolist Movement in Literature* (1899) and
from which Eliot would borrow in formulating his own esthetic.
Obviously it was this same tradition that presented itself to the
young Faulkner.

In 1914 Faulkner had begun a friendship with Phil Stone, back
from Yale University, that was to be one of the important associa-

17

tions of his life as a writer. "Our families had been friends for a generation," Stone says, "and I knew who he was all right, but, as a boy he was almost four abysmal years younger than I was. So I didn't know, or care, much about him until the summer of 1914." At this time Faulkner was painting a little and writing verse. Stone lent him books from his own library — Keats, Swinburne, the new Imagist poets, Conrad Aiken, Sherwood Anderson, the Russian novelists. He also lent him books on esthetics and philosophy, but these were always returned with the margins as clean and untouched as when Stone handed the books to him.

With the entry of the United States into World War I, Faulkner made the rounds of army recruiting stations. Despite his gorging himself on bananas, he was turned down as underweight. Finally New Haven friends of Stone secured a place for him in the Royal Flying Corps, and Faulkner went to Toronto, Ontario, as a cadet. He became an honorary second lieutenant on December 22, 1918, the date of demobilization, and relinquished his commission on the following day. Within a short time he was back home.*

In Oxford, Faulkner sometimes wandered about barefoot, sporting an overseas cap, wide army trousers, and a monocle. This latter item won him the title Count. A few years later, in 1925, writing for the *Double Dealer*, Faulkner admitted that he had toyed with being an eccentric young genius:

My mental life at that period was so completely and smoothly veneered with surface insincerity — obviously necessary to me at that time, to support intact my personal integrity — that I cannot tell to this day [he was now 28!] exactly to what depth [Swinburne] stirred me, just how deeply the footprints of his passage are left in my mind. . . . I read and employed verse, firstly, for the purpose of furthering various philanderings in which I was engaged, secondly, to complete a youthful gesture I was then making of being different in a small town.

Faulkner also had periods, somewhat later, of being the clean-shaven young man wearing an army shirt without tie or coat, and,

* Faulkner did crack up a training plane during his period in the corps, but he was not, despite the legend, shot down in France. Nor did he serve overseas.

later still, of being a dandy, wearing a Vandyke, carrying a cane, being modishly garbed in a light gray hat, with suit to match, and chamois gloves. What the town probably did not see was that beneath the poses was an ironical mind trying to understand itself as well as the community.[2]

His several years at the university, first as a student, then as postmaster, were also a period of being an interesting "character." Faulkner enrolled as a special student in September 1919. During two semesters he studied English, receiving a D and an F; Spanish, two B's; and French, two A's. In November 1920 he withdrew.

That same year Faulkner, at the invitation of Stark Young, went up to New York City. Young had been reared near Oxford, and had taught at the university there. He returned each summer to see his father. Through Phil Stone he knew Faulkner as early as 1914. During Young's subsequent visits, he says, "Bill would bring his poems to read."

Faulkner arrived in New York with forty dollars, having spent sixty for his railway fare. Young was out of town, and for a week Faulkner lived alone, waiting for his return. Then, he says, "I moved in on Young. He had just one bedroom so I slept on an antique Italian sofa in his front room. It was too short. I didn't learn until three years later that Young lived in mortal terror that I would push the arm off that antique sofa while I slept. Stayed with Young until he suggested I better get something to do. He helped me to get a place at Lord and Taylors. I worked in the book department until I got fired. Think I was a little careless about making change or something. Then I came on home."[3]

Stark Young's account of the New York trip is largely the same as this, but with enough difference in emphasis to merit noting: "Finally in the summer of 1920, after the World War, I found [Faulkner] at Oxford in a rebellious mood. Despite the kindness of his parents, and so on, he wanted another sort of life; and I suggested that he come to New York and sleep on my sofa till Miss Prall, a friend of mine, manager of the bookshop in Lord and Taylor's corner, could find him a place there and he could find a room. He did both. (How — for the record again — different that homely denim sofa, bought at a sale, was from that of the interviews: an antique I so preciously feared would be ruined by the wild young genius!) The rest of the data is that Miss Prall married Sherwood Anderson and went to live with him in New Orleans, Bill Faulkner drifted back South and to New Orleans, where through Miss Prall he had a special road open to Sherwood." [4]

For the next two years Faulkner did odd jobs around the campus. One building especially, the law school, was once pointed out as owing its black painted roof and steeple (from which he swung by a rope) to Faulkner. During these months he drove a Ford runabout. In 1922 he bought a red Buick roadster, thanks to his elevation to the office of postmaster for the university station.

As postmaster, Faulkner quickly became a figure of legend. He was a founder of the Bluebird Insurance Company, which insured students against failing grades. The size of the premium, according to an advertisement run in the *Mississippian*, the campus weekly, was arrived at by considering the experience and knowledge of the professor and the size of the class, then dividing both by the student's ignorance. Because of the high premiums charged for most English courses, several younger members of that department retaliated with a huge bold-faced advertisement in the next issue which offered for sale stock in the Midnight Oil Company and printed testimonial letters including one from "Count Wilhelm Von Faulkner, Marquis de Lafayette (County), Post-master General (Retired)."

Faulkner's conscientiousness as postmaster was not notable. Students protested the slowness with which their public servant put down his book, often a Russian novel, before serving them, and the Baptist preacher angrily protested finding several copies of *Baptist Records* in the trash can. The U.S. government was obliged, in 1924, to relieve the postmaster of his duties. He is said to have submitted the following as his letter of resignation: "As long as I live under the capitalistic system I expect to have my life influenced by the demands of monied people. But I will be damned if I propose to be at the beck and call of every itinerant scoundrel who has two cents to invest in a postage stamp. This, sir, is my resignation." [5]

This same year saw the publication of *The Marble Faun*, a collection of poems. Stone later wrote that he had put up the money to pay the Four Seas Company of Boston for publishing it in order to get Faulkner before the public. "I don't think they ever did print the thousand copies they were supposed to publish. I also bought a number of these copies and had Faulkner autograph them for various people and tried to sell them to these people." [6] On the occasion of the awarding of the Nobel Prize, Stone could still say somewhat bitterly: "I still have a few copies for which some of our prominent Oxonians, who now proudly claim his acquaintance, would not then pay a dollar and a half." There seem to have been few or no reviews of it, although in a letter or two to Stone, Harriet Monroe admitted, undoubtedly under pressure from the young poet's patron, that the work was promising. It was about this time that Faulkner one day, walking toward his father's house, told Stone that he was afraid little would come of his attempts to become a writer.

After his dismissal as postmaster, Faulkner, with the money he had saved, planned to go to Europe by way of New Orleans. Once in New Orleans, however, he stayed for about six months, getting to know Sherwood Anderson and other members of the writing colony there. In his *Memoirs* Anderson thus describes his first sight of Faulkner:

I first saw Bill Faulkner when he came to my apartment in New Orleans. You will remember the story of Abraham Lincoln's meeting with the Southern commissioners, on the boat, on the Potomac in 1864. The Southern commissioners had come to try to negotiate some sort of peace and among them was the Vice-President of the Confederacy, Alexander Stephens. He was such a small man and wore a huge overcoat. "Did you ever see so much shuck for so little nubbin?" Lincoln said to a friend.

I thought of the story when I first saw Faulkner. He also had on a big overcoat, it being winter, and it bulged strangely, so much that at first glance I thought he must be in some queer way deformed. He told me he intended to stay for some time in New

The Tangled Fire of William Faulkner

Orleans and asked if in the meantime, while he was looking for a
place, he could leave some of his things with me. His "things"
consisted of some six or eight half gallon jars of moon liquor he
had brought with him from the country and that were stowed in
the pockets of the big coat.

The two men quarreled frequently, but apparently made up
quickly. One of their disagreements was over Faulkner's absurd
contention, at least as Anderson related the incident, that mulattos
could not reproduce. "The result of such a cross is like a mule. It
can't breed its own kind," he said, and when I laughed, he grew
angry and accused me of being a damn Yank. . . . It may be we
both had been drinking. We separated, each walking off alone
and each turning to swear at the other."

The differences between them, the absurdity of this quarrel
aside, arose in part from their being so unlike in temperament.
According to Stark Young, "Sherwood and Elizabeth cooled off
toward Bill, very markedly. He says he never understood just what
it was about." Several reasons why Anderson felt strongly about
Faulkner might be inferred. The character Dawson Fairchild,
obviously Anderson, in *Mosquitoes*, is treated sympathetically but
not with admiration. In the introduction Faulkner wrote for William Spratling's *Sherwood Anderson and Other Creoles*,[7] he paro-
died Anderson's style:

First, let me tell you something about our Quarter, the Vieux
Carre. Do you know our quarter, with its narrow streets, its old
wrought-iron balconies and its southern European atmosphere?
An atmosphere of richness and soft laughter, you know. It has a
kind of ease, a kind of awareness of the unimportance of things
that outlanders like myself — I am not a native — were taught to
believe important. So it is no wonder that as one walks about the
quarter one sees artists here and there on the shady side of the
street corners, sketching houses and balconies. I have counted as
many as forty in a single afternoon, and though I did not know
their names nor the value of their paintings, they were my
brothers. And in this fellowship where no badges are worn and no
sign of greeting is required, I passed them as they bent over their
canvasses, and as I walked onward I mused on the richness of our
American life that permits forty people to spend day after day
painting pictures in a single area comprised in six city blocks.

22

Period of Apprenticeship

When this young man, Spratling, came to see me, I did not remember him. Perhaps I had passed him in the street. Perhaps he had been one of the painters at whose easel I had paused, to examine. Perhaps he knew me. Perhaps he had recognized me when I paused, perhaps he had been aware of the fellowship between us and had said to himself, "I will talk to him about what I wish to do; I will talk my thought out to him. He will understand, for there is a fellowship between us."

But when he came to call on me, I did not remember him at all. He wore a neat business suit and carried merely a portfolio under his arm, and I did not recognize him. And after he had told me his name and laid the portfolio on the corner of my desk and sat opposite me and began to expound his plan to me, I had a kind of vision. I saw myself being let in for something. I saw myself incurring an obligation which I should later regret, and as we sat facing one another across my desk, I framed in my mind the words with which I should tell him No. Then he leaned forward and untied the portfolio and spread it open before me, and I understood. And I said to him, "What you want me for is a wheelhorse, is it?" And when he smiled his quick shy smile, I knew that we should be friends.

We have one priceless universal trait, we Americans. That trait is our humor. What a pity it is that it is not more prevalent in our art. This characteristic alone, being national and indigenous, could, by concentrating our emotional forces inward upon themselves, do for us what England's insularity did for English art during the reign of Elizabeth. One trouble with us American artists is that we take our art and ourselves too seriously. And perhaps seeing ourselves in the eyes of our fellow artists, will enable those who have strayed to establish anew a sound contact with the fountainhead of our American life.

The volume itself is a good-humored, kidding view of the writers and artists in the French quarter. The final illustration is of Spratling and Faulkner sitting at a table painting and writing and drinking. On the wall are a shotgun and a sign reading "Viva Art." Beneath Faulkner's chair are three gallon jugs of corn liquor.

Perhaps the chief reason for Anderson's feelings about Faulkner was that the latter's reputation in certain circles quickly surpassed his own. There is a story, told by Irving Howe in his study of Anderson, of a party given by the *Nation* to honor Anderson, and of Faulkner's coming late and greeting his old friend pleasantly before moving to a table of his own, where he was followed by most of the guests, leaving Anderson smiling abjectly to himself. Among his confidants Anderson was known to speculate rather bitterly about Faulkner's bantam cock qualities, moodiness, and compulsiveness, attributing them to his unusual smallness (he is a little over five feet) and to his inconspicuous success with the ladies.

Faulkner's view of Anderson, while amused, seems less vindictive: "He's dependable, you can trust him to take the children to Sunday School safely. But he's got a glossy coat and a little sporting blood." [8]

Anderson's first impressions of Faulkner, which are now a part of the legend, are suggested by the character David, the young southern poet, in "A Meeting South." [9] David is described as "very small and delicately built," with a lame foot, always in possession of a huge bottle of corn whisky. He is of English descent, his father operates a plantation over in Alabama, and he had joined the Royal Air Force, proved to be a first rate flier, been shot down and severely wounded (two legs broken, one in three places, and the bones in his face badly splintered). Because he wanted to leave the hospital, David had told the doctors the nerves in his face and foot no longer hurt. Actually they pained continuously, preventing his sleeping except under the deadening effects of the corn whisky. In the early part of the tale we see David: "The slight limp, the look of pain that occasionally drifted across his face, the little laugh that was intended to be jolly, but did not quite achieve its purpose. . . ."

All of this is close enough to what Anderson wrote about Faulkner in other places to encourage one to read it as biography. None of the men who have known Faulkner in Oxford, however, have commented on his suffering continually, and he himself indicated that he had discovered the delights of whisky as early as his high school days, quite apart from its medicinal properties.

Through Anderson, Faulkner became associated with Julius Weis Friend and John McClure, the editors of the *Double Dealer*, which was or would soon be publishing many of the young writers,

Period of Apprenticeship

like Hemingway, Crane, Wilson, Tate, Ransom, and Warren, who
were to become important figures. Faulkner contributed quite a
few pieces to the magazine, and learned something of the ways
of literary Bohemia. Anderson helped him get a job on the *Times
Picayune*, for which he wrote a series of impressionistic feature
articles, "Mirrors of Chartres Street." At Anderson's suggestion
Faulkner also tried his hand at a novel, *Soldiers' Pay*, which was
written in six weeks. Anderson liked to claim that it was sent to
Liveright with his recommendation even though he had not read
a word of it. The dedication of *Sartoris* — "To Sherwood Anderson,
through whose kindness I was first published" — suggests that
Faulkner remained grateful to the older writer.

The work Faulkner contributed to the *Double Dealer* has been
collected in the volume entitled *Salmagundi*, edited by Paul
Romaine.[10] In these vignettes and poems and in the half-autobio-
graphical, half-critical sketch of the current literary scene Faulkner's early reading is quite as clear as it had been in "L'Apres Midi
d'un Faune." He says, as we noted earlier, that he had discovered
Swinburne at the age of sixteen and had read him "for the purpose
of furthering various philanderings"; his "concupiscence waning,"
he had read him not for sex, for there is no sex in Swinburne, but
for his "eroticism in form and color and movement." The vignettes
suggest readings in Ernest Dowson. Thus of Magdalen: "Was
there love once? I have forgotten her. Was there grief once? Yes,
long ago. Ah, long ago." But at least one of the poems, "The Lilacs,"
makes it perfectly clear that the young poet from Mississippi was
reading the author of "The Love Song of J. Alfred Prufrock":

Yes, you are right:
One should not die like this,
And for no cause nor reason in the world.

One should not die like this.
His voice has dropped and the wind is mouthing his words
While the lilacs nod their heads on slender stalks,
Agreeing while he talks,
Caring not if he is heard, or is not heard.
One should not die like this. . . .

25

The Tangled Fire of William Faulkner

Half audible, half silent words
That hover like grey birds
Above our heads.

I hear their voices as from a great distance . . . Not dead
He's not dead, poor chap; he didn't die . . .[11]

This is the voice of the new generation, echoing the 1890s but learning to express a newer and more personal sense of betrayal and defeat.

"Mirrors of Chartres Street," the pieces for the *Times Picayune* Sunday edition, are amateur writing, but viewed retrospectively they suggest the direction which Faulkner's talent was taking.[12] Complementary to his apparently cynical and sometimes supercilious looking at the actualities of New Orleans street life is a vision of the world as high romance. The first piece ends with this: "And one thought of Caesar mounting his chariot among cast roses and the shouts of the rabble, and driving along the Via Appia while beggars crept out to see and centurions clashed their shields in the light of golden pennons flapping across the dawn." All the pieces suggest that Faulkner has an eye for people out of the common run of respectability, the down and out, race track sharpies, small-time gangsters, street peddlers, and eccentrics of many varieties. They suggest a good ear but an as yet unperfected talent for catching characteristic phrasing or idioms.

Two pieces in particular, "Sunset" and "The Kingdom of God," foreshadow later characters and subjects. The former is the pathetic story of an ignorant Negro who wants to go home to Africa, is cheated into taking a boat across the Mississippi from New Orleans to Algiers, and after being terribly victimized by his own imagination is killed. The latter is primarily concerned with an idiot in love with a flower:

The idiot still clutched his broken narcissus, weeping bitterly; and while the officer held his wrist the brother hunted about and found a small sliver of wood. String was volunteered by a spectator, who fetched it from a nearby shop; and under the interested eyes of the two policemen and the gathering crowd, the flower stalk was splinted. Again the poor damaged thing held its head erect, and the loud sorrow went at once from the idiot's soul. His eyes were like two scraps of April sky after a rain, and his drooling face was moonlike in ecstacy.

One of the pieces refers specifically to the poetry of Robert Frost, and at least two imply a considerable interest in the technique of the plastic arts. A brief reference to Vorticism is important in the light of Faulkner's later preoccupation with the principle of simultaneity in his fiction, or with what Joseph Frank has labeled "spatial form." If Faulkner knew enough of the theory that was being propagandized by Wyndham Lewis and Ezra Pound to discuss it in relation to light and shade in painting, presumably he knew enough of its literary applicability to have been influenced by it, even though it would probably be going too far to say anything more than that the germs of many of his characteristic devices are in the Vorticist manifestoes, whatever use, if any, Faulkner consciously made of these manifestoes.

Soldiers' Pay is a "lost generation" novel. Donald Mahon, dying from injuries received as a pilot in the British Air Force, returns to his home town in Georgia. His father, an Episcopal clergyman of somewhat relaxed views, and his fiancée, believing he had been killed, are unprepared for his return and shocked by his scarred face and inability to remember clearly, if at all, his earlier life. En route home he is befriended by Margaret Powers, a young war widow, and an enlisted man named Joe Gilligan. Both continue to help him; and Mrs. Powers, out of a sense of having failed her first husband, marries Lt. Mahon in a vain attempt to further his recovery after it is clear that his fiancée, Cecily Saunders, does not intend to marry him. After Mahon's death, Margaret Powers Mahon refuses to marry Gilligan, whom she loves, because "All the men that marry me die" within a year. "I'm too young to bury three husbands." Patriotism, the title implies, is meaningless in a world of selfishness and inevitable defeat.

Many characters flit in and out of the action, but it is Januarius Jones, who comes like a satyr out of the bushes at the edge of the story, who most sustains the Swinburnian and *fin de siècle* mood. His face is described as a "round mirror before which fauns and nymphs might have wandered when the world was young," and his eyes as "yellow, obscene and old in sin as a goat's." Most of Jones' time is spent in pursuit of eligible (and ineligible) females. He is interrupted during one pursuit — he is literally running — for a literary conversation with Mrs. Mahon and Gilligan:

"Perhaps Mr. Jones was merely preparing to write a poem. Living it first, you know," Mrs. Mahon offered. Jones looked at her sharply. "Atalanta," she suggested in the dusk.
"Atalanta?" repeated Gilligan, "what —"
"Try an apple next time, Mr. Jones," she advised.
"Or a handful of salt, Mr. Jones," added Gilligan in a thin falsetto.

Jones is frequently described as a "fat satyr." And the rector too, although a far more sympathetically drawn character, belongs to the knowing and disenchanted world of Anatole France or James Branch Cabell. He lives in his "dream of the world," tends his roses, and expects little from his religion —

"Circumstance moves in marvellous ways, Joe."
"I thought you'd a said God, reverend."
"God is circumstance, Joe. God is in this life. We know nothing about the next."

At the end of the novel, he and Joe Gilligan stand outside a Negro church, "listening, seeing the shabby church become beautiful with mellow longing, passionate and sad. Then the singing died, fading away along the mooned land inevitable with tomorrow and sweat, with sex and death and damnation; and they turned townward under the moon, feeling dust in their shoes."

To the *fin de siècle* and impressionist tradition Faulkner owes also much of the self-consciously elegant (sometimes stiff) style of *Soldiers' Pay*. Thus of a young woman caught in a storm: she ran "across the lawn toward the house before the assaulting battalions of rain. Her long legs swept her up and onto the veranda as the pursuing rain, failed, whirled like cavalry with silver lances across the lawn." Or this of a walk at night:

Gilligan rose in effusive negation. After a while the quiet tree-tunnelled street became a winding road, and leaving the town behind them they descended and then mounted a hill. Cresting the hill beneath the moon, seeing the world breaking away from them into dark, moon-silvered ridges above the valleys where mist hung slumbrous, they passed a small house, sleeping among climbing roses. Beyond it an orchard slept the night away in symmetrical rows, squatting and pregnant. "Willard has good fruit," the divine murmured.

It is notable that the setting of *Soldiers' Pay* is Georgia, not Mississippi, and that there is in it almost nothing of the subjects that were later to occupy Faulkner in his stories of Jefferson and Yoknapatawpha County. But there is a hint or two. There are brief suggestions of the terrible poverty and sadness to which the Negroes are subjected, and there are flashes of his later impatience or even deep uneasiness with southern Christianity:

The Baptist minister, a young dervish in a white lawn tie, being most available, came and did his duty and went away. He was young and fearfully conscientious and kindhearted; upright and passionately desirous of doing good: so much so that he was a bore. But he had soldiered after a fashion and he liked and respected Dr. Mahon, refusing to believe that simply because Dr. Mahon was Episcopal he was going to hell as soon as he died.

But a sense of reality is infrequent in *Soldiers' Pay*. The novel is determinedly world-weary and sophisticated, and the impulses of Margaret Powers Mahon, Gilligan, and Dr. Mahon toward normal responses are not allowed seriously to upset the conventions of the genre to which the novel belongs.

Faulkner's six months or so in New Orleans had been fruitful. He had written *Soldiers' Pay*, done pieces for the *Double Dealer*, worked on the *Times Picayune*, and begun a new novel. In June 1925, accompanied by Spratling, he shipped for Europe on the freighter West Ivis, working in the engine room and on deck. En route he had time to experiment, unsuccessfully he felt, with sonnets, which he disposed of overboard before reaching Genoa. "Made me feel clean," he said.

Faulkner later said he didn't learn very much from this European trip, which was mostly in Italy and France. "At that time the French were impoverished, the Germans naturally servile. I didn't find too much." But he got material for several short stories: "Mistral," "Divorce in Naples," and perhaps "Carcassonne."

He was back in New York by March 1926, when *Soldiers' Pay* was to be released. He signed a contract with Liveright for *Mosquitoes*, and, after a visit in Oxford, went to Pascagoula, near Biloxi, Mississippi, to write it.

The reviewers treated *Soldiers' Pay* with respect. The *New York Times* said "a deft hand" had woven a "narrative of mixed and frustrated emotions," the *Baltimore Sun* predicted it would still be read when most of the year's books "are meditating dustily on inaccessible shelves," and Louis Kronenberger found it a "rich compound of imagination, observation and experience." But it sold only twenty-five hundred copies. And *Mosquitoes*, published the following June, sold a mere twelve hundred copies, again despite reviews that were mostly favorable.

Mosquitoes belongs self-consciously to the 1920s and probably was influenced by Aldous Huxley. The plot is negligible, seeming to exist solely as occasion for endless dull talk. Mrs. Maurier, a wealthy and frustrated New Orleans widow, assembles, with the unasked assistance of her flip teen-aged niece, a somewhat diversified group for a yachting party — among them, an unsophisticated but ardent young couple casually brought along by the niece, several artists and writers from the French quarter, an Englishman who has been convinced by advertisements that all Americans are constipated, and the futile Mr. Taliaferro, a department-store buyer who becomes the butt of practical jokes because of his ridiculous attempts at seduction. Except for the niece's sudden elopement with the steward, and her being bitten severely by mosquitoes in the swamp and having to return to the yacht, there is almost no action; even the elopement affords an excuse for long discussions of the mores of the younger set:

A few years ago a so called commercial artist (groan, damn you) named John Held began to caricature college life, cloistered and otherwise, in the magazines; ever since then college life, cloistered and otherwise, has been busy caricaturing John Held.

Or of the differences between the physical composition of women like Anna Held and Eva Tanquay, "with shapes like elegant parlor-lamp chimneys," and the boylike figures of the flapper generation:

"Where," he continued, "are the soft bulging rabbitlike things women used to have inside their clothes? Gone, with the poor Indian and ten cent beer and cambric drawers. But still, they are kind of nice, these young girls: kind of like thin monotonous flute music or something."

Faulkner has almost none of Huxley's talent for the novel of ideas, either for sustained intellectualizing or for playing off idea against idea. Like Gordon, the sculptor, who wanted to escape from the yachting party, Faulkner does not seem happy with this subject; he seems to be throwing off whatever it means or represents to him by satirizing its frustrations and castigating its blasé and sophisticated posings. Despite occasional claims to the contrary, it is not true that he is an able satirist of sophistication. Satire that is razor-edged usually implies some partial involvement in, some margin of affection or liking for, the situations satirized. Faulkner is not really involved in what little there is of sophisticated action in *Mosquitoes*; he is merely brushing it aside.

One might guess that Gordon is modeled to some extent on Faulkner himself, or upon his ideals, for Gordon alone seems largely made of the flint of which Faulkner's later protagonists are usually composed; he alone seems to have Faulkner's sense of man suffering: "Only an idiot has no grief: only a fool would forget it. What else is there in the world sharp enough to stick to your guts." Yet Gordon never develops as a character, and with his great red beard, his huge torso, and his grim view of the non-artist world he comes perilously close to being a stereotype.

Dawson Fairchild, the novelist modeled on Sherwood Anderson, is more completely realized as a character, even though what one comes to know about him seems to have no particular relevance to the rest of the novel.* In one passage where Faulkner is unmis-

* Faulkner puts into Fairchild's mouth the first of the tall tales that will appear in his fiction. He has Fairchild tell a story, for example, of a man and sheep turning into fish. In speaking of his New Orleans period and acquaintance with Anderson, Faulkner recalls Anderson as a man dedicated to the purity of his art. He also comments on the tall tales which he and Anderson worked up together, some of which found their way into *Mosquitoes*.[13]

takably discussing Anderson there is an interesting comment on Anderson's affirmation of things American and his conscious effort to isolate them:

"His writing seems fumbling, not because life is unclear to him, but because of his innate humorless belief that, though it bewilder him at times, life at bottom is sound and admirable and fine; and because hovering over this American scene into which he has been thrust, the ghosts of Emerson and Lowells and other exemplifiers of Education with a capital E. who, 'seated on chairs in handsomely carpeted parlors' and surrounded by an atmosphere of half calf and security, dominated American letters in its most healthy American phase 'without heat or vulgarity,' simper yet in a sort of ubiquitous watchfulness. A sort of puerile bravado in flouting while he fears," he explained.

Again,

"But he lacks what they had at command among their shelves of discrete books and their dearth of heat and vulgarity — a standard of literature that is international. No, not a standard, exactly: a belief, a conviction that his talent need not be restricted to delineating things which his conscious mind assures him are American reactions."

Undoubtedly a little vignette on Anderson as he appeared to the young Faulkner could be drawn from *Mosquitoes*, but the groping honesty suggested by the portrait does not seem to be intended as a commentary on the sophisticated elements of the story as a whole.[14]

Faulkner's powers of rhetoric and the *fin de siècle* connections of that rhetoric are evident throughout the novel, as in passages like this: "The *Nausikaa* dreamed like a gull on the dark water"; or this: "But the moon was still undimmed, bland and chill, affable and bloodless as a successful procuress, bathing the yacht in quiet silver; and across the Southern sky went a procession of small clouds, like silver dolphins on a rigid ultramarine wave, like an ancient geographical woodcut." Usually he is not satisfied with a little richness of effect; he insists on continuing, after the manner of Edgar Saltus or James Branch Cabell or Carl Van Vechten, until the metaphors are too obviously the work of artifice, like multi-colored and highly polished cut glass. For example:

The violet dusk held in soft suspension lights slow as bell-strokes, Jackson square was now a green and quiet lake in which abode lights round as jellyfish, feathering with silver mimosa and pomegranate and hibiscus beneath which lantana and cannas bled and bled. Pontalba and cathedral were cut from black paper and pasted flat on a green sky; above them taller palms were fixed in black and soundless explosions. The street was empty, but from Royal street there came the hum of a trolley that rose to a stagger-ing clatter, passed on and away, leaving an interval filled with the gracious sound of inflated rubber on asphalt, like a tearing of endless silk.

Faulkner's next novel, *Sartoris*, was deliberately written to sell, but Horace Liveright declined to publish it. After many rejections it was accepted by Harcourt, Brace and published in February 1929. It sold fewer than two thousand copies.

Like Donald Mahon of *Soldiers' Pay*, Bayard Sartoris, the pro-tagonist of *Sartoris*, is a returned aviator, an offspring of the world-weary young men in the *fin de siècle* tradition:

His head was clear and cold; the whiskey he had drunk was com-pletely dead. Or rather, it was as though his head were one Bayard who lay on a strange bed and whose alcohol-dulled nerves radiated like threads of ice through that body which he must drag forever about a bleak and barren world with him. "Hell," he said, lying on his back, staring out the window where nothing was to be seen, waiting for sleep, not knowing if it would come or not, not caring a particular damn either way.

Bayard is presented as embittered by the death in a dogfight of his twin brother John. Repeatedly he risks his life, riding a danger-ous horse, madly racing an automobile, finally meeting his death in testing an airplane that no sensible pilot would take off the ground. He leaves behind him a widow, Narcissa Benbow Sartoris, and a young son, born the day he is killed. Bayard is one of Faulk-ner's compulsive and violently driven heroes, but the reasons for his violence, although suggested, are not very clear.

Bayard's blood is apparently atavistic; to it he owes his blind, headlong courage. On the final page of the novel his actions are accounted for in these terms:

The music went on in the dusk softly; the dusk was peopled with ghosts of glamorous and old disastrous things. And if they were just glamorous enough, there was sure to be a Sartoris in them, and then they were sure to be disastrous. Pawns. But the Player, and the game He plays. . . . He must have a name for His pawns, though. But perhaps Sartoris is the game itself — a game outmoded and played with pawns shaped too late and to an old dead pattern, and of which the Player himself is a little wearied.

If Bayard is a spirit left over from a heroic past, he seems to know little of that past or what it meant. He seems bent on destroying himself more out of an unmotivated "lost generation" world-weariness than out of the rejection of a world that has no interest in the grand manner and headlong heroics. The last-page explanation of Bayard has the air of being an appeal to a costume world.

Sartoris is especially interesting as a source book for later Faulkner stories. Banker Bayard Sartoris, for example, who meets his death from heart failure in the last of young Bayard's mad automobile drives, reappears in *Light in August, Absalom, Absalom!* and other stories. Huge Dr. Peabody, man of folksy wisdom, reappears in *As I Lay Dying*. Byron Snopes, a bookkeeper, and Flem Snopes, vice-president in the bank, reappear in the Snopes saga. In a later short story, "There Was a Queen," Byron Snopes steals the obscene letters he had written to Narcissa Benbow in *Sartoris*, and Flem's dishonesty as city manager of the light and water plant is developed in "Centaur in Brass." Horace Benbow, Narcissa's brother, who has been called one of Faulkner's "good weak heroes," reappears in *Sanctuary* and in other stories as well. In *Sartoris* Benbow has an affair with Belle Mitchell, a married woman. When we meet him in *Sanctuary* we learn that he has been married to Belle for ten years.

Perhaps more significant than these interrelationships are Faulkner's characterization of the McCallums — pine hill farmers or "countrymen," a class treated with respect and admiration in later stories — and his treatment of a backwoods Negro family in sympathetic rather than humorous and stereotyped terms. These figures and episodes take him closer to the realities of his later themes and subjects. A passage in *Sartoris* about the Mississippi mule suggests how close Faulkner was getting to grim and violent realities and necessities without having broken with the mannerisms of the sophisticated and esthetic tradition in which he had begun his career:

Round and round the mule went, setting its narrow, deerlike feet delicately down in the hissing cane-pith, its neck bobbing limber as a section of rubber hose in the collar, with its trace-galled flanks and flopping, lifeless ears and its half-closed eyes drowsing venomously behind pale lids, apparently asleep with the monotony of its own motion. Some Homer of the cotton fields should sing the saga of the mule. . . . Father and mother he does not resemble, sons and daughters he will never have; vindictive and patient (it is a known fact [this is a statement Faulkner repeats in "Old Man" in almost the same terms] that he will labor ten years willingly and patiently for you, for the privilege of kicking you once), solitary but without pride, self-sufficient but without vanity; his voice is his own derision. . . . Alive, he is haled through the world, an object of general derision; unwept, unhonored, and unsung, he bleaches his awkward and accusing bones among rusting cans on lonely hillsides while his flesh soars unawares against the blue in the craws of buzzards.

The dignity and pathos of his subject here almost but not quite overcome the pose, the will to rhetoric, of the clever young writer.

The Christmas morning visit of young Bayard at the Negro cabin is almost fully successful as a touching human scene involving the pathos and shame of white and Negro relationships. And being such, it contrasts with the clever but too easy comedy of the earlier sections in which the Negro, although not without guile, is the ingenuous grown-up child:

Old Bayard snorted violent. "You get that money back and give it to those niggers, or you'll be in jail, you hear?"

"You talks jes' like dem uppity town niggers," Simon told him in a pained tone. "Dat money done been put out, now," he reminded his patron.

35

"Get it back. Haven't you got collateral for it?"

"Is I got which?"

"Something worth the money, to keep until the money is paid back."

"Yessuh, I got dat." Simon chuckled again, unctuously, a satyrish chuckle rich with complacent innuendo. "Yessuh, I got dat, all right. Only I never heard hit called collateral befo'. Naw, suh, not dat."

If *Sartoris* in organization, conception, and rhetoric suggests the self-conscious young writer, it also contains passages which give promise of the full genius of Faulkner's mature prose. For example: "Again the hounds gave tongue in the darkness below them. The sound floated up on the chill air until its source was lost and the very earth itself might have found voice, grave and sad, and wild with all regret." *

When he was halfway through *Sartoris*, Faulkner later said, he developed a new respect for writing: "I discovered that writing is a mighty fine thing; it enabled you to make men stand on their hind legs and cast a long shadow."

---

* The phrase "wild with all regret" appears in Tennyson's "Tears, Idle Tears." Whether Faulkner borrowed it consciously or not is of no great moment, but it does suggest another source of his rhetoric.

Emergence of a Major Writer

THE SOUND AND THE FURY is the work of a major writer. With its appearance it became clear that Faulkner was a committed artist, now writing in the tradition of the modern novel to which Henry James, Joseph Conrad, Stephen Crane, Ford Madox Ford, and James Joyce had contributed.

Faulkner said it took him three years to do the book and that he had "written [his] guts" into it. His discouragement when Harcourt, Brace declined it must have been very great. But Harrison Smith accepted it, thereby winning his lasting gratitude. The book was published under the imprint of Jonathan Cape and Harrison Smith in October 1929.

The story is presented in four sections. The first (dated April 7, 1928) is the timeless interior monologue of Benjy, in which events of the past and present are juxtaposed and interflow. The reader is well into the section before he recognizes that events are dim and shadowy because the narrator of them is an idiot. Although Faulkner has made the sentences a little more orderly than they would actually be in such a mind, the fragmentary nature of Benjy's impressions make the monologue convincing.

The second section (dated June 2, 1910) presents some of the

NOTE: The part of this chapter dealing with *The Sound and the Fury* is reprinted, with modifications, from the original version in *Northern Review*, vol. 6, no. 2 (June–July 1953), by permission of the editor.

The Tangled Fire of William Faulkner

same as well as new events, through the mind of young Quentin Compson at Harvard. It is only after following the weird distortions of his mind for some time that the reader learns that Quentin is so occupied with time because he is getting ready to kill himself.

The third section (April 6, 1928), returning the action to Jefferson, concentrates on the mean-spirited and thieving Jason. Jason's refraction of the story as it relates to him is in a much more simplified idiom, less dreamily stream-of-consciousness than the idiom of Benjy or Quentin.

The final section (April 8, 1928) stays with no single character, although the dominant tone comes from the Negro servant Dilsey, and for the most part maintains an objective and omniscient view of the more recent events, primarily of Caddy's daughter Quentin (named for her uncle) running away with a pitchman from a visiting carnival and taking with her the three thousand dollars Jason accumulated by allowing his mother to believe he had burned the checks Candace sent for the support of her daughter Quentin. The events in the final section, though seen in a broader perspective than those in the earlier sections, are dependent upon what has gone before, and the reader feels he has lived intimately through the anguish, stupidity, and villainy of the Compson family, and is finally watching its destinies move out of the foreground of his consciousness and recede into their place in history or in the reader's other memories.

In part, the story is about the loss of innocence. Faulkner said the story "began with the impression of a little girl playing in a branch and getting her panties wet. This idea was attractive to me, and from it grew the novel."[1] The childhood of the Compson children, although with the usual scuffles and worries and with the symbolic act of Caddy's staining her buttocks in the mud, is a period of natural innocence. To her young and idiot brother Benjy, Caddy always "smells like trees." But after her seduction by Dalton Ames and her calculated marriage to Sydney Herbert Head, the northern banker, Benjy can't "smell trees anymore." The children enter the adult world.

As an appendix for *The Portable Faulkner*, edited by Malcolm

Emergence of a Major Writer

Cowley, Faulkner wrote a history of the Compson family, giving most attention to the generation of Compsons who people *The Sound and the Fury*.[2] Jason III, the father of Quentin, Candace, Benjy, and Jason IV, is a lawyer. Sitting in his office he contemplates the gradual loss of Compson's Mile, the square mile owned by his forebears (a general, a governor, planters, aristocrats) and finds solace in drinking from the decanter on his desk and in writing satiric verses on his fellow townsmen, living and dead. Jason Compson's family is in an advanced state of decay.

It is necessary to ask, then, what thematically Faulkner is saying in *The Sound and the Fury*. The passage in *Macbeth* from which he took the title for his novel is undoubtedly a clue to his intended meaning. Literally, in part it is a tale told by an idiot, but signifying what? Quentin and his obsessions are treated with obvious sympathy, and it could well be that in Quentin one finds the central issue of the novel.

The loss of his sister's honor and his own half-conscious desire for incest with her tend to dominate his mind and to dominate the novel — to have something to do with the decay of the Compson family. In Cambridge, before his suicide, he is seen pondering what he is:

. . . until after the honeysuckle got all mixed up in it the whole thing came to symbolise night and unrest I seemed to be lying neither asleep nor awake looking down a long corridor of grey halflight where all stable things had become shadowy paradoxical all I had done shadows . . . antic and perverse mocking without relevance inherent themselves with the denial of the significance they should have affirmed thinking I was I was not who was not was not who.

Honeysuckle, for Quentin, represents the South and it represents Caddy's sex. Her honor and the traditional preoccupation with personal honor merge. Quentin's desire for incest with Caddy suggests social disorder, a family that is narcissistic. Insistence upon honor and dignity have become extreme, forms of self-love. Living in the midst of decay with the glories of the family's past is living with ghosts.

The Tangled Fire of William Faulkner

Mrs. Compson, for example, doesn't see how God can allow indignities to be heaped upon a lady of her family origins, and she is ashamed of Benjy, changing his name from Maury, her brother's name, to Benjamin. But Dilsey, the old Negress, knows the difference between pretentious pride and dignity; she is willing to be seen publicly with Benjy, to undertake the responsibilities of care and affection for him. When she hears that his name is to be changed, she says: "He aint wore out the name he was born with yet, is he?" Jason IV revolts completely from the family's self-love. Caddy sells herself, turning sharply away from the family and whatever it represents to her; and Quentin, bemused by a pursuit of honor that itself is perverted and diseased, kills himself.

Quentin's mad reveries about incest dramatize a point similar to one made by T. S. Eliot in his essay on Baudelaire: "It is better, in a paradoxical way, to do evil than to do nothing: at least we exist." Not merely family history but religious belief and the fear of time form the antic shadows in Quentin's mind. Echoes from *Hamlet* and other plays hover at the edge of his consciousness. Unlike the present, the past believed in honor, and for many reasons the Compsons were an honorable family. In the past, a Calvinist Jehovah was ready to thunder in the clouds if with an excessive breath a member of the family tarnished the shield of their sacred honor.[3] But Quentin's father tells him it is time (clocks tick, hum, and whir in poor Quentin's head), not God, that he fears: the idea of incest, which he didn't commit, would, however perversely, give him a sense of terrible significance and thereby lift him out of time. The "loud world," as Quentin calls it, believes neither in the sacred individual nor in honor. Incest, Quentin had hoped, would take him back into his own childhood, or, if not that, into an eternity where one was paid the grim respect of being tormented by fire for having fallen from an honorable estate.

Perhaps more than any of Faulkner's other characters, Quentin is the twentieth-century hero, the man of sensibility studying his own identity, searching for significance in a world that is not sure it believes in any. Nor is Quentin sure himself that he believes in any, but the torment of unbelief is great enough to contribute to his suicide. Only Dilsey and her kind who hold simply to the old beliefs live honorably. Of her and what she represents Faulkner wrote a memorable phrase: "They endured."

The Sound and the Fury takes Faulkner deeply into his most characteristic subject matter, his heritage as a southerner, and modern man in search of belief. And it takes him as an artist deeply into the experiments of the twentieth-century novel. It was, of course, a part of the critical code of the impressionist school that a scene be rendered, not reported or narrated. Faulkner is usually faithful to this part of the impressionist code, even to the point of refusing to inject a word or to interpolate a sentence or two which might greatly clarify the meaning of a scene. For example, in Benjy's section of *The Sound and the Fury* there are many scenes comparable to this:

"Hush, Benjy." Caddy said. "Go away, Charlie. He doesn't like you." Charlie went away and I hushed. I pulled at Caddy's dress.

"Why, Benjy." Caddy said. "Aren't you going to let me stay here and talk to Charlie awhile."

"Call that nigger." Charlie said. Charlie came and put his hands on Caddy and I cried more. I cried loud.

"No, no." Caddy said. "No, no."

"He can't talk." Charlie said. "Caddy."

"Are you crazy." Caddy said. She began to breathe fast. "He can see. Dont. Dont." Caddy fought. They both breathed fast. "Please. Please." Caddy whispered.

"Send him away." Charlie said.

"Yes." Caddy said. "Let me go." Charlie went away. "Hush." Caddy said. "He's gone." I hushed. I could hear her and feel her chest going.

There are a few more verbal exchanges between Charlie and Caddy; then in compunction she takes Benjy home and washes her mouth out with soap. Benjy, incapable of drawing the usual inferences, does not realize that Charlie is making advances to Caddy. Her conduct is not discussed in moral or social terms for the simple reason that what the reader sees is what Benjy sees. Similarly, there is a scene in which Benjy burns his hand, but although there is a description of his putting his hand into his mouth and of Dilsey's putting soda on it, the word *burn* is never

41

used. Faulkner is rendering, not reporting. The impressionist novelist, as Ford Madox Ford put it, "renders the world as he sees it, uttering no comments, falsifying no issues and carrying the subject — the affair — he has selected for rendering remorselessly out to its logical conclusion."

In modern literature this doctrine of impersonality or anonymity has of course been very influential.[4] T. S. Eliot has spoken of the poem's being not an expression of but an escape from personality, and E. M. Forster of the sense in which a work of art has its meaning apart from the author. Allen Tate, in a preface to a volume of his poetry, has said that the emotions to be found in the poems were not transcripts of his own feelings but that the poems were structures (presumably tinkered with) which he hopes will be the causes of appropriate experiences in the reader. Such statements are a part of the reaction against the nineteenth-century view that literature is the outpouring of the author's soul, either immediately or recollected in tranquility. Behind the newer doctrine is the belief that the reader is, or should be, interested in the work of art in itself, not as a transcript of its source in the author or as an expression of the author's personality.

For many generations critics have quoted Buffon's "Style is the man," but now they are more likely to reach out for a dictum like Mark Schorer's "Style is the subject." Neither statement is exclusively true, but the latter undoubtedly implies a fuller understanding of the way in which a literary work gets written and a more candid acceptance of the way in which it will shift in its meanings for later generations of readers. Many works written in the twentieth century have deliberately followed the principle that the appropriate style is implicit in the subject matter. The style of *Dubliners*, as Joyce claimed, is appropriately one of "scrupulous meanness," and in *Ulysses* the sentimental talk of Gerty McDowell is hers, not Joyce's; the precise, proper language of Father Conmee is his, not Joyce's; and most obviously the unintellectual, free-flowing bawdiness of Molly Bloom is hers, not Joyce's.*

* In an interview with Henry Nash Smith Faulkner said he had not read *Ulysses*, that the copy of the Paris edition of the novel which he had was

Emergence of a Major Writer

In the following passage Quentin Compson in Cambridge, Massachusetts, is presented thinking his own thoughts, harking back to a conversation he had once had with his father about suicide and his having tried to make his father believe that he and Caddy had committed incest:

. . . it seemed to me that i could hear whispers secret surges smell the beating of hot blood under wild unsecret flesh watching against red eyelids the swine untethered in pairs rushing coupled into the sea and he we must just stay awake and see evil done for a little while its not always and i it doesn't have to be even that long for a man of courage and he do you consider that courage and i yes sir dont you and he every man is the arbiter of his own virtues whether or not you consider it courageous is of more importance than the act itself than any act otherwise you could not be in earnest and i you don't believe i am serious and he i think you are too serious to give me cause for alarm and he i think you wouldnt have felt driven to the expedient of telling me you have committed incest otherwise and i i wasnt lying i wasnt lying and he you wanted to sublimate a piece of natural human folly into a horror and then exorcise it with truth and i it was to isolate her out of the loud world so that it would have to flee us of necessity and then the sound of it would be as though it had never been and he did you try to make her do it and i i was afraid to i was afraid she might and then it wouldnt have done any good but if i could tell you we did

The language is obviously that of Quentin's obsessed and tortured mind, contemplating suicide and recalling the grief and shame of Caddy's affairs and his own attempt to exorcise them. The reader is given no help by an omniscient author; he learns only as much

acquired after he had written *The Sound and the Fury*. He acknowledged that he had heard discussions of Joyce's experiments: "Someone told me about what he was doing, and it is possible I was influenced by what I heard." He also made several comments about his attitudes and methods of working which by implication shed light on his fiction: "There is the first stage when you believe everyone and everything is good. In the second you believe no one is good. Then at last you come to realize that everyone is capable of almost anything — heroism or cowardice, tenderness or cruelty." And he said that the patterns of his novels were not preconceived: "When I started to write *The Sound and the Fury* I had no idea of writing the book it finally became, it simply grew from day to day, and it was not until the book was finished that I realized I had in it the anecdote of the girl who ran away with the man from the traveling show." [5]

as he could if he were looking into Quentin's mind, and he learns it in the idiom in which it there exists.

Again, the vicious, ironic cynicism of Jason Compson is everywhere evident in his language, whether spoken or thought; in the following passage he is thinking of Benjy, his brother:

I could hear the Great American Gelding snoring away like a planing mill. I read somewhere they'd fix men that way to give them women's voices. But maybe he didn't even know what they'd done to him. I don't reckon he even knew what he had been trying to do. Or why Mr. Burgess knocked him out with the fence picket. And if they'd just sent him on to Jackson while he was under the ether, he'd never have known the difference. But that would have been too simple for a Compson to think of. Not half complex enough. Having to wait to do it at all until he broke out and tried to run a little girl down on the street with her own father looking at him. Well, like I say, they never started soon enough with their cutting, and they quit too quick. I know at least two more that needed something like that, and one of them not over a mile away, either.

The reception of *The Sound and the Fury* was not such as to give Faulkner cause for satisfaction in his acceptance by the literary world. Fewer than two thousand copies had been printed, indicating that the publishers themselves had no great expectations for the novel. But with Evelyn Scott's pamphlet, *On William Faulkner: The Sound and the Fury*, he received his first significant critical attention:

William Faulkner has that general perspective in viewing particular events which lifts the specific incident to the dignity of catholic significance, while all the vividness of an unduplicable personal drama is retained. . . . Luster, that marvellously accurately conceived young negro . . . Moral conclusions can be drawn from it as surely as from "life," because, as fine art, it is life organized to make revelation fuller. Jason is, in fair measure, the young South, scornful of outworn tradition, scornful indeed of all tradition, as of the ideal which has betrayed previous generations to the hope of perfection . . . Dilsey provides the beauty of coherence against the background of struggling choice. She recovers for us the spirit of tragedy which the patter of cynicism has often made seem lost.

44

Emergence of a Major Writer

Miss Scott called the novel an "important contribution to the permanent literature of fiction."[6]

Faulkner next — while working nights shoveling coal in a power plant — wrote *As I Lay Dying*, his favorite among his own novels, and dedicated it to its publisher, Harrison Smith. His working hours were from 6:00 p.m. to 6:00 a.m., but from midnight to 4:00 a.m. he wrote, using an upside-down wheelbarrow for a table. *As I Lay Dying* was issued in October 1930. It was written in only six weeks with a dynamo humming in his ears. And it required almost no revision. "Someday," Faulkner said, "I'm going to buy a dynamo and put it in my workroom."[7]

The speed with which *As I Lay Dying* was written bears no relationship to the skill with which it was written. Concentrating on a character at a time, fifteen of them in all, the action is broken into sixty sections. Each character, simultaneously refracting and participating in the forward movement of the story, cuts into its substance and meaning to the degree possible to his consciousness and perception. Plot and character interflow or interact with a naturalness and ease that may be unmatched in modern fiction. If T. S. Eliot was right in saying that American fiction took its first step forward since Henry James in *The Great Gatsby*, then one should be free to say that *As I Lay Dying*, which makes Fitzgerald's technique seem wooden and creaky, was a tremendous stride forward, making possible levels of awareness, a sense of variety, and a saturation of reality that would have delighted Henry James.[8]

As I Lay Dying is Jamesian also in the sense that it does not respect the naturalists' doctrine of faithfulness to historical and social actualities, to documenting a people and a place. The symbolic, stylized journey of *Gulliver's Travels* or *Rime of the Ancient Mariner* is beyond our fact-clogged twentieth-century imaginations — but *As I Lay Dying* is closer to either of them than it would be to a sociological account of dirt farmers in Lafayette County, Mississippi. The journey with Addie Bundren's coffin is absurd. Addie herself "exists" as a stylized view of the human need to be

45

involved and committed. Viewed as we would view our neighbor, she is quite mad. Viewed in relation to certain other characters in the story she is wonderfully human. She is a part of a macabre symbolic action.

Reduced to a simple outline the action of *As I Lay Dying* is this: Addie Bundren, the wife of Anse Bundren, is dying. Cash, her eldest son, is building her coffin. Addie is visited by Dr. Peabody, but she is beyond his help and obviously wants to die. It becomes apparent quickly that Anse is stingy, given to easy self-justification, and eager (despite protestations to the contrary) to have his burdens carried by others. Darl, the second son, is looked on by the neighbors as strange. He has the power to read the thoughts or at least to guess the secrets of members of the family. He knows that Jewel is not Anse's son. From Addie we learn that Jewel is the son of Whitfield, the preacher. And Darl knows that Dewey Dell, the fourth child, is pregnant by Lafe, a neighbor boy, and that she wants Addie to die quickly so that she can have an abortion in Jefferson. Vardaman, the youngest, thinks Peabody has killed his mother. A number of neighbors are also involved in the action, especially Cora Tull and her husband, she as a scatterbrain who sees all her beliefs and actions as having divine authority, he as a put-upon but patient and helpful man.

Presently Addie dies. The funeral journey to Jefferson is a nightmare: The coffin is upset in a swollen stream; Cash's leg is broken —it is coated with cement and thereafter he rides on the coffin; Darl sets fire to Gillespie's barn to destroy the putrescent corpse, but the coffin is saved by Jewel; buzzards follow the corpse; in Mattson the sheriff tells the Bundrens to keep on moving, and a respectable druggist indignantly refuses to sell pills to Dewey Dell; in Jefferson, Addie is finally buried, Dewey Dell is seduced by a soda clerk who pretends to be a doctor, Darl is picked up and sent to an insane asylum in Jackson, and Anse, with a new set of teeth, returns to his waiting family to introduce "a duck shaped woman" with popeyes as the new Mrs. Bundren.

Addie Bundren is the center of the story. The complex relationships between Addie and her neighbors, Anse, Whitfield, and her

children is the story. We live, she believes, by violating our aloneness. Words like *love* and *sin*, which signify the violations, are too
often abused, used meaninglessly. Those who are involved do not
need the words. And those who are not involved, regardless of
the events in which they are caught, do not live meaningfully —
they move through the world like wraiths. The nightmarish funeral
procession from the Bundren farm to Jefferson, brought about by
Addie's grim design to involve Anse at least to the degree of fulfilling a promise, is of course the central action. Presumably the
degree of involvement of each member of the family, Anse, Cash,
Darl, Jewel, Dewey Dell, and Vardaman, is defined in relation
to it.

The section entitled "Addie," recapitulating her life, is the most
explicit statement of the meaning of involvement and of violence
as its sign and symbol. A statement which Addie repeats in various
forms is this: "I could just remember how my father used to say
that the reason for living was to get ready to stay dead a long
time." As a young schoolteacher in the neighborhood of Anse's
farm, she endures the bitterness and frustration of not knowing
what it is she is searching for:

I would look forward to the times when they faulted so I could
whip them. When the switch fell I could feel it upon my flesh;
when it welted and ridged it was my blood that ran, and I would
think with each blow of the switch: Now you are aware of me.
Now I am something in your secret and selfish life, who have
marked your blood with my own for ever and ever.

To escape, she married Anse. "So I took Anse. And when I knew
I had Cash, I knew that living was terrible and that this was the
answer to it."

But Anse did not know the world as she knew it. He lived with
the word *love* without knowing it meant the violation of self.
Addie felt betrayed by Anse. And when she knew she had another
child, Darl, she felt it was Anse's and not hers. Thereafter she
denied herself to Anse. With Whitfield, the preacher, she began a
relationship which she thought would be violation and not words.
She says in explanation of her meetings with him in the woods: "I

believed that the reason was the duty to be alive, to the terrible blood, to the red bitter flood flowing through the land." She saw Whitfield as dressed in the brilliant garments of sin. And to sin was to live. Their child was Jewel. But Whitfield too, as the section in which he rationalizes his actions amply demonstrates, lives with words. Addie gives him up. Out of fairness, "to negative Jewel," as she puts it, she gave Anse Dewey Dell. "Then I gave him Vardaman to replace the child [Cash] I had robbed him of. And now he has three children that are his and not mine. And then I could get ready to die."

Cash and Addie have no need for words, not even the word *love*. Addie says: "I knew that word was like the others: just a shape to fill a lack; that when the right time came, you wouldn't need a word for that anymore than for pride or fear. Cash did not need to say it to me nor I to him, and I would say, Let Anse use it, if he wants to."

Cash lives not with words but with the fact. In the early part of the action, his literal-minded relation to the fact is comic. When he is asked the distance he had fallen from the roof he had been fixing, he says: "Twenty-eight foot, four and a half inches, about." One of the chapters devoted to him is concerned solely with the measurements for the casket which he works on during the final hours of Addie's life. A few moments before her death, he holds a board up to the window for her to see. When she is dead, he pauses, saw in hand, to study her face, paying no attention to the pious mouthings of Anse, then returns to his work. During the journey to Jefferson Cash's leg is broken. He endures the agony of its being coated with cement (because Anse does not want to spend money for a doctor) in order that he may remain with the body of Addie until it is buried. He is loyal to her, working out the tension of their relationship. Cash accepts the violence that is everyone's lot. And he is rewarded by a maturity of sympathy and understanding — he can sympathize with Darl and speculate intelligently on the line between sanity and insanity — of a kind denied to the other members of the family. His is a reasonable relation between the fact and the word.

Emergence of a Major Writer

Jewel, as Darl insists in order to torment him, has no father. The child of Addie's violence, he lives, at least until she is buried, involved in the fury of his origins. No one in the action says so little. His relationship with the rest of the family is almost that of an outsider. The only one he is committed to is Addie. If he could have it as he wished, "It would just be me and her on a high hill and me rolling the rocks down the hill at their faces, picking them up and throwing them down the hill, faces and teeth and all by God until she was quiet." There is a sputtering, explosive violence to Jewel's speech as well as to his action. He curses frequently, usually at members of the family. Appropriately he works long hours for many nights to buy a horse (a descendant of the violent Texas ponies described in "Spotted Horses," later to be incorporated into *The Hamlet*). The horse appears to be a symbol of the violence to which a fatherless son of Addie is heir. Darl, who torments him, says, "Jewel's mother is a horse." And Addie's tears over her son, who knows life as she knows it, are understandable simply in terms of her sympathy for him. When Darl sets fire to Gillespie's barn, it is Jewel who, suffering painful back burns, drags out Addie's coffin. Only after Addie is buried and Darl has been taken to an asylum does Jewel's anguish subside, as though he had accepted his obligation to live with Addie's blood until it was tamed and quieted.

Darl's compulsion to torment Jewel arises from his knowing that Jewel is Addie's child, born of her fury, and that she had considered his own birth an outrage. "I cannot love my mother," he says, "because I have no mother." Cash was born in her knowledge that life is bitter and terrible; he had violated Addie's aloneness as Anse never had. With Cash, her "aloneness had been violated and then made whole again by the violation." Darl sees to it that Jewel is away when Addie dies. And he sets fire to the barn to prevent Addie's being buried in Jefferson, as she wished, thus repudiating her as she had him. Presumably Darl's uninvolvement, his remoteness from event or person, is intended by Faulkner to be the reason for his psychic perceptions and finally for his insanity. Some of

49

The Tangled Fire of William Faulkner

Darl's speculations are poignant beyond those of any other figure in the story:

I don't know what I am. I don't know if I am or not, Jewel knows he is, because he does not know that he does not know whether he is or not.

How often have I lain beneath rain on a strange roof, thinking of home.

The theme of the novel in part is the obligation to be involved, with involvement implying a commitment to violence. Presumably Anse's inability to be involved causes the children of Addie's indifference to him, Dewey Dell and Vardaman, to be something less than human, one characterless, the other close to idiocy. But the logic of these relationships seems something less than inexorable, causing the theme of the novel to be imprecise. Put another way, Addie's being deeply moved by her view of the world but indifferent to three of the children of her own flesh offends our sense of verisimilitude.

Vardaman is only a little less pathetic than Darl. His weakness of mind and the shock of her death somehow cause him to associate a bloody, chopped up fish with his mother. Like an eerie refrain through the story, he says, "My mother is a fish." Vardaman is a victim of Anse's ineffectuality and of Addie's terrible commitments.

Dewey Dell is more like Anse than are the other children. She is also enough like Addie though to know the world as bitter: "I feel like a wet seed wild in the hot blind earth." But she cannot give herself to violence or accept it: "I don't know what [worry] is. I don't know whether I am worrying or not. Whether I can or not. I don't know whether I can cry or not. I don't know whether I have tried to or not." She does not accept the responsibility for her act with Lafe. She is incapable of fully acknowledging her pregnancy. She is even eager, as Darl says, for Addie's death: "You want her to die so you can get to town: is that it?" And Moseley, the respectable druggist from whom she tries to buy pills, tells her that "life wasn't made to be easy on folks." Her hatred for Darl — because he knows and might reveal her secret — is as intense as

Jewel's hatred for him. It is Dewey Dell who tells Gillespie that
Darl fired the barn. And with Jewel she attacks Darl physically
when the officers come to take him to Jackson.

Anse, Whitfield, and Cora Tull make a great display of their
involvement — all three, but especially the latter two, in Christian
terms. For the satisfaction of his desires, Anse depends upon his
family and his neighbors, either upon their sympathy or upon his
taking advantage of them. Peabody knows the reason Anse didn't
call him to attend Addie was because he feared the cost. When
Addie dies, Anse responds characteristically: "God's will be done,"
he says. "Now I can get them teeth." He takes from Cash's pocket
the money Cash has saved to buy a phonograph and he trades
Jewel's horse without Jewel's permission or knowledge. This is a
sample of his self-justification:

> Anse stands there, dangle-armed. "For fifteen years I ain't had a
> tooth in my head," he says. "God knows it. He knows in fifteen
> years I ain't et the victuals He aimed for man to eat to keep his
> strength up, and me saving a nickel here and a nickel there so my
> family wouldn't suffer it, to buy them teeth so I could eat God's
> appointed food. I give that money. I thought if I could do without
> eating, my sons could do without riding. God knows I did.

Later he takes from Dewey Dell the ten dollars Lafe had given her
for the pills she was unable to buy. He even borrows the spades to
dig the grave for Addie. In the final scene of the novel we see Anse
coming down the street, the rest of the family except Darl waiting,
with his new teeth and his new wife:

> "It's Cash and Jewel and Vardaman and Dewey Dell," Pa says,
> kind of hangdog and proud too, with his teeth and all, even if he
> wouldn't look at us. "Meet Mrs. Bundren," he says.

Preacher Whitfield holds a high place among the despicable
creatures Faulkner has created. Whitfield so lives with the righteous, high-sounding phrases of the pulpit and the professional
servant of God that he appears not to know where the fact, the
wrong, or the obligation stops and the word begins. The section
called "Whitfield" is done with the economy of an uncompromising
irony. Radiant with his own self-rightousness, Whitfield models his

repentance on the Prodigal Son: "Anse, I have sinned. Do with me as you will." But when he learns that, Addie having died, no one need know of his sin, he says: "I have sinned, O Lord. Thou knowest the extent of my remorse and the will of my spirit. But He is merciful; He will accept the will for the deed, Who knew that when I framed the words of my confession it was to Anse I spoke them, even though he was not there. It was He in His infinite wisdom that restrained the tale from her dying lips as she lay surrounded by those who loved." Whitfield's words are always adaptable to selfish purposes.

Cora Tull, a scatterbrain who never suffers a moment of self-doubt, is treated humorously; as, for example, in her conversation with her husband when he is telling her how Darl jumped, leaving Cash on the wagon when it was upset in Tull's swollen stream:

"And you're one of the folks that says Darl is the queer one, the one that ain't bright, and him the only one of them that had sense enough to get off that wagon. I notice Anse was too smart to been on it a-tall."

"He couldn't 'a done no good, if he'd been there," I said. "They was going about it right and they would have made it if it hadn't a-been for that log."

"Log, fiddlesticks," Cora said. "It was the hand of God."

"Then how can you say it was foolish?" I said. "Nobody can't guard against the hand of God. It would be sacrilege to try to."

"Then why dare it?" Cora says. "Tell me that."

"Anse didn't," I said. "That's just what you faulted him for."

"His place was there," Cora said. "If he had been a man, he would 'a been there instead of making his sons do what he dursn't."

"I don't know what you want, then," I said. "One breath you say they was daring the hand of God to try it, and the next breath you jump on Anse because he wasn't with them." Then she begun to sing again, working at the wash-tub, with that singing look in her face like she had done give up folks and all their foolishness and had done went on ahead of them, marching up the sky, singing.

This is Addie's account of Cora:

And so when Cora Tull would tell me I was not a true mother, I would think how words go straight up in a thin line, quick and harmless, and how terribly doing goes along the earth, clinging to it, so that after a while the two lines are too far apart for the same person to straddle from one to the other; and that sin and love and fear are just sounds that people who never sinned nor loved nor feared have for what they never had and cannot have until they forget the words. Like Cora, who could never even cook.

The theme of *As I Lay Dying*, then, would seem to invite the dividing of people into those who accept the bitterness and violence of living and those who do not. In terms of the immediate family, the choices to be made are usually clear: Anse merely pretends involvement with Addie alive and with his promise to bury her in the plot of her folks in Jefferson; Cash fulfills his obligation to his mother and earns his right to speculate about human motives and conduct; Jewel fulfills his, persisting in the terrible effort to get to Jefferson, sacrificing his horse, and endangering his life. In these figures the theme seems consistently worked out. It seems confused, or at least more devious, in the cases of Darl, Dewey Dell, and Vardaman. Addie lives as one doomed and as one dooming her children, fulfilling her obligation to the "bitter blood boiling through the land."

Faulkner's first major works, *The Sound and the Fury* and *As I Lay Dying*, developed themes that were to persist in novel after novel. The former is about a family suffering from disbelief in the old virtues or from their decay. The novel is Faulkner's wasteland, his statement that men cannot live as automatons, without the traditional virtues. Though the world at large no longer affirms the fact, man is a spiritual creature. If man does not live with dignity, self-respect, responsibility, and love, he will go the way of the Compsons. The other novel says, by implication, that these virtues have little to do with one's social class. Man is separate from the beasts. He lives in a harsh world, and he should recognize it as such. But he has his compensations. He can know a sense of his own significance and being by violating his aloneness, by accepting what he has to accept to be decently human.

Faulkner is not an orthodox Christian, but his beliefs are without question from the Christian doctrines. His Nobel Prize speech contains a sentence which, though it is quite different in tone from the language in either *The Sound and the Fury* or *As I Lay Dying,* might be used as a legend for a volume containing both of them: "He is immortal, not because he alone among the creatures has an inexhaustible voice but because he has a soul, a spirit capable of compassion and sacrifice and endurance."

—————————————— 4

Sanctuary and Popular Success

In February 1930 the *Wilson Library Bulletin* ran a biographical sketch of Faulkner, characterizing him as a strong-minded young man, who despised New York City and much preferred living in Oxford. "Physically he is short in stature, but he is hardily constructed. His hair and eyes are very black. His nose broken once is aquiline and his expression sharp and keen." His next book, the *Bulletin* said, is to be *Sanctuary*.

Sanctuary was the turning point in Faulkner's reputation, or notoriety, as a writer. Before writing it, he later said, he asked himself what would sell at least ten thousand copies, then "chose what I thought was the right answer and invented the most horrific tale I could imagine and wrote it in about three weeks and sent it to Harrison Smith." Smith answered at once, "Good God, I can't publish this. We'd both be in jail." But Smith later sent him the galleys and Faulkner, being ashamed of the writing, revised it as much as he could.

Under the title "The Cult of Cruelty" Henry Seidel Canby featured *Sanctuary* on the first page of the *Saturday Review of Literature*.[1] One of the New Humanists, Alan Reynolds Thompson, analyzed the cult of cruelty for the *Bookman* in even more

note: This chapter is reprinted, with modifications, from the original version in *Faulkner Studies*, vol. 1, no. 3 (Fall 1952), by permission of the editor.

sober terms than those of Mr. Canby. Parlor Freudians found in it a topographical map of ids, egos, and less easily mentioned entities. Corey Ford, the satirist, devoted a section to it in *In the Worst Possible Taste* (with a drawing by Covarrubias of Faulkner as a popeyed boy in shorts standing in a bin full of corncobs). Another caricature, "Mr. Faulkner Is Visited by the Muse," a dream of monsters, enormous axes, and so on, appeared shortly in the *Bookman*. A pamphlet, *Pseudo-realists*, by "Junius Junior" was devoted exclusively to *Sanctuary*. Paramount bought the story and released it as a movie entitled "The Story of Temple Drake," starring Miriam Hopkins and Jack La Rue.° In the movie, Popeye became a character named Trigger, and Temple became a virtuous maiden, temporarily bemused by the power of evil, who shoots him, then testifies at the trial that Trigger had shot Tommy. In the novel, of course, she falsely accuses Lee Goodwin.

In 1932 *Sanctuary* was reissued by Modern Library, in which it has had a notable history of sales. It was published in three English editions, and it was translated into French in 1933 and into Spanish in 1934. An article by H. P. Lenormand, a French dramatist, made explicit what it was in Faulkner that appealed so readily to the French: "Faulkner was immediately recognized as belonging to the tradition of Poe, because of his power, and the means he uses, to transcend reality: his insistent brush-strokes, his repetition, his

---

° It was with the publication of *Sanctuary* that Faulkner first came to the attention of Hollywood, and since then he has, from time to time, spent periods of several months there writing scripts. Legends seem to grow around Faulkner even more quickly than they do about other novelists, and his Hollywood experiences provide two of the better tales.

The first, told by Roark Bradford, is a story which has circulated widely about Faulkner's first visit to Hollywood.² The legend goes like this: The Hollywood moguls were in awe of the man who wrote about idiots, rape with a corncob, fantastic funeral journeys, and so on, and they decided to awe him in turn with Hollywood grandeur. Nunnally Johnson was assigned the job and given an elaborate office, one hundred feet long, on three levels, linked by flights of marble stairs. After Faulkner entered and introduced himself, there was a painful silence. He then reached into his pocket for a flask, took a long drink, and placed the flask on the desk for Johnson. Three weeks later the studio sleuths found Faulkner and Johnson in an Okie camp, still drunk.

Nunnally Johnson, whom I asked to comment on the legend, modified it in these terms: "Roark Bradford's account of my meeting with Faulkner was

minuteness of detail — so many procedures turning their back on realism, but leading miraculously to a world of nightmares. This technique of hallucination and this constant exhalation of fright naturally place Faulkner in the succession of the master of horror." [3]

Faulkner was now famous, and at least *Sanctuary* was widely read. A parody of the ways Alexander Woollcott, P. G. Wodehouse, and Faulkner would treat the story of Jack and Jill appeared in the *Saturday Review* in December 1936.[4] It begins:

The rotting fields of tomatoes sent up a stench that filled the lungs with decay; one could taste the putrid slime of the crawling things that ate their way through the spoiled crops. . . .

Years later at a football game when Faulkner shrewdly predicted the right play, Saxe Commins said, "Now you'll be known as the grandstand quarterback." Faulkner replied, "No, I'll always be known as the corncob man!"

Once when asked whether Popeye, the vicious gangster, had any "human prototype," Faulkner answered, "No, he was symbolical of evil. I just gave him two eyes, a nose, a mouth, and a black suit. It was all allegory." Faulkner was, it would seem, influenced by

a little elaborate. It is true that we went immediately into conviviality, but it was far from as extensive as Bradford described it. . . . Bill arrived with a pint of bourbon in a paper sack and another inside. He's a very independent fellow with a bottle and so he managed to rip his thumb opening the one he carried exteriorly, but since we had a wastebasket handy, he permitted the blood to drip there while we carried on our discussion. In the end we went out to continue our discussion in a saloon."

Faulkner himself has given the actual facts behind another legend, told to illustrate his childlike innocence, of his having said he could work better at home than in a Hollywood office and the executive's saying, "All right, go home to work," thinking Faulkner meant Santa Monica, whereas he meant Oxford, where he proceeded to go. "That story," Faulkner says, "is better than mine. I had been doing some patching for Howard Hawks on my first job. When the job was over, Howard suggested I stay on and pick up some of that easy money. I had got $6,000 for my work. That was more money than I had ever seen, and I thought it was more than was in Mississippi. I told him I would telegraph him when I was ready to go to work again. I stayed in Oxford a year, and sure enough the money was gone. I wired him and within a week I got a letter from William B. Hawks, his brother and my agent. Enclosed was a check for a week's work, less agent's commission. These continued for a year with them thinking I was in Hollywood."

newspaper stories which featured Popeye Pumphrey, a Memphis racketeer, elaborating them for his own artistic purposes.*

Horace Benbow, after talking with Temple Drake in Miss Reba's cathouse, where Popeye has taken her after the rape with the corncob, thinks this to himself as he walks down a Memphis street:

> Better for her if she were dead tonight . . . For me, too. He thought of her, Popeye, the woman [Ruby Goodwin, Lee Goodwin's common-law wife], the child, Goodwin, all put into a single chamber, bare, lethal, immediate and profound: a single blotting instant between the indignation and the surprise. And I too; thinking how that were the only solution . . . Removed, cauterised out of the old and tragic flank of the world.

There is only a thin margin of decency possible in such a world, and the only intelligent attitudes are the pessimistic calm of Ruby Goodwin and the fatalistic commiseration and kindness of Horace.

In this story, as in many others, Faulkner is hard on Baptist righteousness. Horace Benbow is the only one in the Christian community of Jefferson who tries to help Goodwin, falsely charged for the murder of Tommy, the poor half-wit whom Popeye had shot when Tommy tried to help Temple. Miss Jenny, the ninety-year-old aunt, who appears earlier in *Sartoris*, is seen here as cynical but calm and broadminded; she says, "You won't ever catch up with injustice, Horace." Narcissa, Horace's sister and the widow of Bayard Sartoris, and the other righteous ladies force Ruby and her ill child to leave Horace's house and later the hotel.

Clarence Snopes, the Mississippi state senator, is sheer opportunist, willing to sell information to Horace or to Temple's father, Judge Drake, whoever will give him the more profit. And the district attorney, Eustace Graham, like most of the politicians in Faulkner, manipulates human beings strictly for his own advantage as a vote-getter. He invites the lynching of Goodwin merely because it is convenient for him to sway the jury by appeal-

---

* It has been said that *Sanctuary* is based on a bit of autobiography told to Faulkner and a companion in a night club in the 1920s by a girl who had had experiences with an impotent gangster similar to the experiences of Temple and Popeye.[5]

ing to their basest prejudices: "You have just heard the testimony of the chemist and the gynecologist — who says that this is no longer a matter for the hangman, but for a bonfire of gasoline." Gowan Stevens, Narcissa's twenty-five-year-old suitor, is described as a plumpish, irresponsible young man with a swaggering air. He indulges in alcoholic orgies, occasionally remembering that University of Virginia men should be able to hold their liquor. After one orgy he leaves Temple Drake to the mercies of Popeye and his colleagues in crime at the Goodwin place in Frenchman's Bend. The students at the university are uniformly without manners or consideration for their elders or each other. Horace's wife, whom he had taken from another man, is unfaithful to him.

The evil in *Sanctuary* is of two sorts — that inherent in the human creature, and that resulting from modern mechanism and our having lost an easy relationship with nature, the woods, the birds, the seasons. The evil inherent in human nature, in "the tragic flank of the world," is caught in part by an almost casual pattern of nature or flower imagery, the heaven-tree, the grape, and the honeysuckle; and the evil of a mechanized, vulgar, meretricious world inhabited by most of the characters is caught in images that are metallic and dehumanized.

The heaven-tree stands at the corner of the jailyard where Lee Goodwin and a Negro wife-murderer are imprisoned. The Negro sings mournful spirituals while awaiting his death by hanging, and he complains that he should not be hanged because he is the "bes ba'yton singer in nawth Mississippi." Goodwin is afraid to say that Popeye killed Tommy because then Popeye would have him killed, probably by a shot through the jail window. The heaven-tree is an ironical symbol of the melancholy and despair of the two prisoners. The Negro's voice can be heard in the evenings "coming out of the high darkness where the ragged shadow of the heaven-tree which snooded the street lamp at the corner fretted and mourned." At one point the blossoms are described thus: "The last trumpet shaped bloom had fallen . . . they lay thick, viscid underfoot, sweet and oversweet in the nostrils with a sweetness surfeitive and moribund, and at night now the ragged shadows of full fledged leaves pulsed upon the barred window in the shabby rise and fall." Many of the words used in the description relate to the two men in the jail and to the story as a whole: *trumpet shaped* suggests Judgment Day; *thick, viscid, surfeitive,* and *fallen* their soon-to-be-decaying bodies; and *shabby* their hopelessness and the cheap and dishonest motives of many involved in their fates.

Not even Horace, the one good man in the story, is free from the evil. Grape and honeysuckle become involved in his repressed or half-conscious preoccupation with the body of Little Belle, his stepdaughter. Her "voice would be like the murmur of the wild grape itself." Little Belle, self-centered and quite capable of dissimulation, was a part of the "conspiracy between female flesh and female season," the spring. Again, "He was thinking of the grape arbor . . . darkening into the pale whisper of her white dress, of the delicate and urgent mammalian whisper of that curious small flesh which he had not begot and in which appeared to be vatted delicately some seething sympathy with the blossoming grape."

Later the grape imagery recedes before Horace's awareness of the smell of honeysuckle, which in *The Sound and the Fury,* as here, is identified with the sweetness, richness, and evil powers of sex. Walking to his home shortly after hearing Temple tell of her rape at Frenchman's Bend, Horace smells honeysuckle. "He opened the door and felt his way into the room and to the light. The voice of the night — insects, whatever it was — had followed him into the house; he knew suddenly that it was the friction of the earth on its axis, approaching the moment when it must decide to turn on or to remain forever still: a motionless ball in cooling space, across which a thick smell of honeysuckle writhed like cold smoke." Later he sees Little Belle's picture on the dresser in his room. As he studies the face, he sees her enveloped in "slow-smoke-like tongues of invisible honeysuckle. Almost palpable enough to be seen, the scent filled the room and the small face seemed to swoon in a voluptuous languor. . . ." His excitement increases as the images in his fantasy change and he sees her carried on a roaring train through a dark tunnel, the shucks whispering madly beneath her, as they had beneath Temple. Then he realizes that he has identified Little Belle with Temple, that she is involved in a world "across which a thick smell of honeysuckle writhes like cold smoke." What has happened to Temple might happen to her.

The second, more persistently developed, pattern of imagery is that of an urbanized, metallic, inhuman existence. The historical origins of this existence are not explored. It is merely accepted as a form of evil superimposed on the evil inherent in the human condition "on a motionless ball in cooling space." Popeye has eyes like "two knobs of soft black rubber," his face is like "the face of a wax doll set too near the fire and forgotten," his fingers are like steel "but cold and light as aluminum," and he has that "vicious depthless quality of stamped tin." His hat is "all angles, like a modernistic lampshade." Popeye is afraid of the woods and uneasy with or frightened by the sounds or the quietness of the countryside.

But it is not merely Popeye, born a syphilitic and pervert, who is inhuman. The people in the world around him are depersonalized or inhuman in some degree. The people in Jefferson who listen to the old simple ballads "of bereavement and retribution and repentance" hear them "metallically sung, blurred, emphasized by static or needle — disembodied voices blaring from imitation wood cabinets or pebble grain horn mouths. . . ." The blind father of Goodwin, with eyes like "phlegm clots" or "dirty yellowish clay marbles," seems an almost wraith-like symbol of the unseeing or amoral world, whether of Popeye, Narcissa, or Clarence.

Eyes are frequently described in *Sanctuary* but never as warmly or decently human. When Lee Goodwin takes a coat from Temple in a semidarkened room, their eyes are described thus: "Her eyes were quite wide, almost black, the lamp light on her face and two tiny reflections of his face in her pupils like peas in two inkwells." The doctor who attends Temple at Miss Reba's has eyes "like little bicycle wheels at dizzy speed; a metallic hazel." Coed acquaintances of Temple are once seen studying one of their group with "eyes like knives."

The Tangled Fire of William Faulkner

The descriptions of Temple are done in terms appropriate to her. Temple's speech is "parrot-like," and on one occasion her grimace is like "porcelain." The passage in which she is seen in court picks up earlier descriptions and develops them into this image of her:

From beneath her black hat her hair escaped in tight red curls like clots of resin. The hat bore a rhinestone ornament. Upon her black satin lap lay a platinum bag. . . . Above the ranked intent faces white and pallid as the floating bellies of dead fish, she sat in an attitude at once detached and cringing. . . . Her face was quite pale, the two spots of rouge like paper discs pasted on her cheek bones, her mouth painted into a savage and perfect bow, also like something both symbolical and cryptic cut carefully from purple paper and pasted there.

But the tinny, cheap, debauched, and vulgar world of Popeye and Temple is not restricted to their talk or dress or manners; it is a part of the very landscape they *see*. During their trip to Memphis they experience "a bright, soft day, a wanton morning filled with that unbelievable soft radiance of May, rife with a promise of noon and of heat, with high fat clouds like gobs of whipped cream floating lightly as reflections in a mirror, their shadows scudding sedately across the road."

Incidental descriptions of other characters, such as Snopes, Judge Drake, and even Miss Reba, extend this pattern of imagery and metaphor. Snopes is called the pie-faced man, or, in more detail, is said to have a "face like a pie took out of the oven too soon." Even Snopes' sartorial effects and dress are related to a mechanical order: "the whole man with his shaved neck and pressed clothes and gleaming shoes emanated somehow the idea that he had been dry-cleaned rather than washed." Several times Judge Drake's mustache is referred to as hammered silver — "like a bar of hammered silver against his dark skin." Miss Reba's cheap jewelry and beer tankard are described in terms that suggest a vulgar metallic world. Finally, even the coeds are seen as having "painted small faces and scant bright dresses like identical artificial flowers."

62

Sanctuary and Popular Success

These patterns of imagery suggest that Faulkner gave this novel closer attention in the writing than he said, or implied, he did. It is episodic, sometimes introducing scenes that in the main are irrelevant, like the affairs of Fonzo and Virgil Snopes or the beer guzzling of Uncle Bud, and much of the irony is too pat; but the mood and tone are generally uniform. A part of this mood or tone emanates from the highly connotative language that Faulkner on occasion employs. The words, quoted above, used to describe the blossoms of the heaven-tree suggest the method, the way in which a word catches a specific or concrete detail and rises as an overtone, relating itself to a larger situation or even to the whole story.

Faulkner is willing to employ such connotations consciously. He is even willing to coin terms or to force connotations by using words, not obviously metaphorical, which require careful interpretation. The following passage, concerned with Temple's first experience of Miss Reba's cathouse, has been criticized as an example of careless diction, willful ambiguities, and preciousness:

The narrow stairwell turned back upon itself in a succession of *niggard* reaches. The light, falling through a thickly curtained door at the front and through a shuttering window at the rear of each stage, had a weary quality. A spent quality; *defunctive,* exhausted — a protracted weariness like a vitiated backwater beyond sunlight and the *vivid noises* of sunlight and day. There was a *defunctive odor* of irregular food, *vaguely alcoholic,* and Temple even in her ignorance seemed to be surrounded by a *ghostly promiscuity of intimate garments,* of discreet whispers of flesh stale and oft-assailed and *impregnable* behind each silent door which they passed.

The italicized words and phrases are those cited as evidence that Faulkner lays about him like "a bright sophomore." Yet if read with something like the attention one gives to poetry each of the expressions is readily understandable: *niggard* suggests short and cramped, with the connotations of meanness and miserableness; *defunctive* describes a light that is gray, used-up, almost dead; *vivid noises* is an example of synesthesia, an adjective usually restricted to *things* being applied to *sound*; *vaguely alcoholic* plainly

63

suggests that gin or whisky was a part of the meal and the odor of
it lingers; in the phrase *ghostly promiscuity of intimate garments,*
ghostly implies the recent or former presence of the women and
promiscuity applied to garments is patently a transferred epithet;
no real difficulty arises with *impregnable* if one recognizes that it
means not physical but spiritual impregnability, the irony of so
much physical union without love.

The cathouse, incidentally, is a good symbol of the world Faulkner is castigating, a world in which money and self-interest pre-
clude or destroy affection or love, and a world in which sex writhes
like "cold smoke." In *Sanctuary* the former world is presented in
part through the imagery of the brassy, the metallic, the inhuman,
and the latter through the imagery of the grape and honeysuckle.
Probably *Sanctuary* is overwritten, seeming unreal in the way an
expressionistic play, which pushes too hard against its symbols,
seems unreal, and without doubt it is extremely melodramatic; but
the esssential truth it contains, realized in shocking scenes and
through a highly wrought idiom, is clearly implied. As a novel it
is far above the level of "potboiler," the term Faulkner himself
applied to it.[6]

                                                                    5
──────────────────────────────────

These Thirteen and Other Stories

R<small>EVIEWING</small> <small>ERICH</small> <small>REMARQUE'S</small> *The Road Back* for the *New Republic*,[1] Faulkner delivered himself of two critical dicta: One, it is a writer's privilege to put into a character's mouth better speech than an actual person would be capable of, but only if the speech relates to the character's own situation (he should not sound like the voice of a chorus). Second, a personal experience, no matter how vivid it may be, cannot be transferred directly to a work of fiction — "somewhere between the experience and the blank page and the pencil, it dies."

As for Remarque's book itself, Faulkner was of two minds. He found it moving but essentially sentimental, probably created for the western trade, "to sell among the heathen like colored glass." Conceivably Faulkner, with two of his best novels behind him, felt sufficiently free from the sentimentality of his own American war generation to be critical of it. If so, he was not deterred from publishing some of his own more sentimental stories, *Idyll in the Desert* and a few of the war stories in *These Thirteen*.[2]

Idyll in the Desert was issued by Random House in a special edition of four hundred copies.* It is a morbid tale, told rather

* In October 1931 Faulkner went up to New York, staying at the Algonquin, for the release of *Idyll in the Desert*. Knowing he was being sought as a new celebrity, Faulkner hid out with Hal Smith, his publisher. En route South again, he traveled with Smith and Anthony Buttitta, a young editor

jerkily, about the fate of a woman who leaves her two children and wealthy husband to nurse a lover younger than she by ten years. The setting is the desert in the Southwest. After she contracts tuberculosis from him, the lover leaves her. Living alone in their cabin, she wastes away. While being taken in a baggage car to a hospital in California, she sees the young man with his bride on a station platform! He looks at her, but does not recognize her. At the next station she is dead.

Surprisingly few of Faulkner's short stories had appeared in magazines, and after the publication of *Sanctuary*, he had the pleasure of resubmitting, with price tags attached, stories previously turned down by editors.[4] A check of *The Best Short Stories of the Year*, however, shows that Edward J. O'Brien thought highly of Faulkner's short fiction, selecting it regularly for his annual volumes and only occasionally missing the significant worth of a story.

These Thirteen is similar to *Sartoris* in that it finds its subject matter in the disenchantment of the war generation as well as in the past and present of Jefferson. Several of the stories, only tan-

of *Contempo*, a North Carolina little magazine. The three of them stopped off at the University of Virginia for a meeting of thirty-odd southern writers. In an article about the meeting for the *Harold Tribune* Emily Clark devoted a paragraph to Faulkner: "William Faulkner attended meetings and parties intermittently, and was beyond doubt, the focal point of every gaze, since this new and dazzling light of American letters had never before been in Virginia, and leaves Mississippi only once in four or five years. His publisher, Harrison Smith, also down for the day, remarked that Mr. Faulkner, who never can be persuaded to take his metropolitan reviews with fitting seriousness, was, like all good Southerners, both serious and flattered in his acceptance of an invitation from the University of Virginia. This exponent of horror beyond all imaginable horrors, a gentle, low-voiced, slight young man, on his first evening astonished his admirers and interested spectators by murmuring, while conversations and argument raged around him, the placating phrase, 'I dare say,' at infrequent intervals; and by gently crooning 'Carry Me Back to Old Virginia,' in an automobile between Charlottesville and Farmington."[3]

Faulkner and a group with whom he was traveling stopped for a day or two at the University of North Carolina. During their stay the group visited a class devoted to problems in the technique of fiction. At the end of the lecture, Mr. Phillips Russell, the instructor, asked Faulkner if he would like to make any remarks. The author of *The Sound and the Fury* rose and said that during his entire writing career he had never for a moment worried about problems of technique!

gentially if at all concerned with the war, add to one's sense of Faulkner as would-be cosmopolite and self-conscious artist.

None of the four war stories, which Faulkner in his *Collected Stories* (1951) has grouped under the title "The Wasteland," is particularly distinguishable in its harsh subject matter or unqualifiedly bitter irony from war stories written by John Dos Passos, Ernest Hemingway, or Hervey Allen. "Crevasse," except for a few passages of Faulknerian description, might have been written by any of them. "Ad Astra" tells of the deadness of spirit, the hopelessness experienced by Bayard Sartoris and his companions in France on the night of the armistice. All of them talk of their personal isolation, their disbelief: "And outside in the chill November darkness was the suspension, the not quite believing, not quite awakened nightmare, the breathing spell of the old verbiaged lusts and the buntinged and panoplied greeds."

John Sartoris dominates "All the Dead Pilots," a somewhat incoherent story, mostly about the ridiculous, almost mad competition between Sartoris and his commanding officer for the attention of a young French tart. Presumably the episodes are intended to explain the lost generation, "all the old pilots, dead on the eleventh of November, 1918." Many pilots have lived on into the era of "saxophone girls and boys with slipstream-proof lipstick and aeronautical flasks," and so forth, but they, having so often faced death and violence, carry death within them. The atmosphere of "All the Dead Pilots" is similar to the atmosphere created by such plays as *What Price Glory?* and *Journey's End*.

"Victory," a story as blatantly ironical as its title, tells of a God-fearing young Scot whose war experiences turn him into a killer. He also experiences the irony of having learned to ape the ways of the upper class, into which he had been thrust by virtue of being an officer, but this class, as well as the whole society, rejects him. White haired, dead-eyed, and bitter, he is reduced to selling matches on the street. "Victory" is perilously close to being a formula story, and is saved, insofar as it is, only by the wonderful early passages in which a sense of the soldier's God-fearing Scotch family is evoked with economy and wit.

The Tangled Fire of William Faulkner

Among the best of the stories are "That Evening Sun," "Dry September," and "A Rose for Emily," all of which represent the special quality of Faulkner.* There is terrible suffering and pathos in "That Evening Sun," in Nancy Mannigoe's knowing that her husband is going to kill her. Accepting the inevitability of her murder she sits with her door open and says, "I just got tired. . . . I just a nigger. It ain't no fault of mine." The scene and the story as a whole suggest not merely a local history of exploitation, guilt, and ignorance, but human frustration, white and black, at the bleakest point of hopelessness and despair. Only slightly less powerful is "Dry September," a story of the wretchedness, the sadism, and the shame of the man who has helped to lynch a Negro. "A Rose for Emily," probably Faulkner's best short story, is surely one of the most grim yet touching stories in all English literature of the disaster that may attend a denial of natural affection. †

"Hair" is not, for Faulkner, a very good story, but it is interesting as the first in which his subject is a "countryman," here a barber who was the son of a tenant farmer. Like Byron Bunch of *Light in August,* he is gentle, almost ascetic, hard working, and dedicated. Despite the small margin of satisfaction in his life and the almost grim quality of the little pleasure achieved, he has dignity and stature, and Faulkner is undoubtedly saying it is a "successful life." (Incidentally, Gavin Stevens, the Jefferson lawyer, appears briefly in this story.) "Hair" is unlike the "wasteland" stories, closer to Faulkner's special subject matter and to his own grim affirmations.

* Some of the materials in these stories are carried over to later ones. For example, the murder of Nancy Mannigoe, threatened in "That Evening Sun," is referred to as an accomplished fact in *The Sound and the Fury.* But Nancy, resurrected, appears again in *Requiem for a Nun* as the reformed dope fiend and whore who forces Temple to live the moral life.

† "A Rose for Emily" is, I think, misinterpreted by those critics who see the story as a conflict between the values of the Old South and the new order, business-like, pragmatic, self-centered. It can't be read in these terms because the Old South and the new order are merely a part of the flavor and tone of the story, *not* the poles of conflict. The theme is that a denial of normal emotions invites retreat into a marginal world, into fantasy. The severity of Miss Emily's father was the cause of her frustrations and her retreat. The past becomes a part of her fantasies, just as the present does. It is incidental that her relationship to the Old South makes her a part of the town's nostalgia; it was the nostalgia, not her being a "lady," which caused her to be

Two other stories also take Faulkner closer to one of his local subjects, the Chickasaw Indians of an ante-bellum Mississippi. "A Justice" tells of the connivings of Ikkemotube, or Doom, who murdered his way into the Manship or head of the tribe. The narration, which is listened to by twelve-year-old Quentin Compson (another boy, Ike McCaslin, will hear the story later in "The Old People," a section of *Go Down Moses*), concerns the paternity of Sam Fathers, part Negro, part Indian. Quentin is too young to understand Doom's unsuccessful efforts to keep Crayfishford, Sam's father, away from the wife of a slave, Sam's mother, or to understand the irony of Doom's soothing the ire of the cuckolded slave by commenting on the attractive yellowness of the child, saying "I don't see that justice will darken him any."

"Red Leaves" is more specifically concerned with the implacable cruelty but also the serenity of the Indians, and suggests that the white man and slavery (the Indians ape the white men by keeping slaves they don't really want) have destroyed their easy relationship with a luxuriant and game-rich earth. The Negro suffers at their hands too, and in this story one is pursued through the brush because as the body servant of a dead chief he must be buried with him. After a madly furious attempt to escape through the swamps he is caught. Just what Faulkner means the story to symbolize is not completely clear, but in part he must be saying that slavery disturbed, even for the Indian, the proper relationship with the land and that the tortured shadow of the Negro has hovered over Mississippi from its earliest history.

treated reverently by the town's board when she refused to acknowledge her taxes; presumably even ladies paid their taxes in the Old South. If the conflict is between the two orders it seems curious indeed that Miss Emily would choose Homer Barron, Yankee, amoral, and without loyalty, as her beloved. And her murder of the new order, Homer Barron, is the reverse of what actually happened: the destruction of the old order by the new. The story is simple enough when read as an account of Miss Emily's becoming mad as a consequence of her frustrations, the denial to her of normal relationships. That the Old South, which as a physical presence (in its houses, memories, and so on) lingers in the new order and in doing so seems unreal, has its parallel, obviously, in Miss Emily, who was most strangely detached from reality. But this is a parallel only — it is not the dramatic pull or struggle that composes the action.

The Tangled Fire of William Faulkner

The general situation of "Mistral," one of the three remaining stories, is that of Gide's *Symphonie Pastorale,* and the dialogue as well as the body-and-time-haunted world it evokes is Hemingway's. Only in occasional descriptions, when the language seems almost transported, does "Mistral" suggest Faulkner. "Divorce in Naples," on the other hand, has Faulkner's stamp, especially in the taut yet sympathetic humor with which a young sailor's sexual initiation in an Italian port city is described. "Carcassonne" is hardly a story, in that it has no development or plot, but it is interesting for what appears to be an autobiographical assertion, Faulkner's ambition to create out of words "something bold and tragical and austere" —

I want to perform something bold and tragical and austere he repeated, shaping the soundless words in the pattering silence *me on a buckskin pony with eyes like blue electricity and a mane like tangled fire, galloping up the hill and right off into the high heaven of the world.* Still galloping, the horse soars outward; still galloping, it thunders up the long blue hill of heaven, its tossing mane in golden swirls like fire. Steed and rider thunder on, thunder punily diminishing: a dying star upon the immensity of darkness and of silence within which, steadfast, fading, deepbreasted and grave of flank, muses the dark and tragic figure of the Earth, his mother.[5]

Miss Zilphia Gant, a short story published in a single volume by the Texas Book Club, would appear to be an early effort, certainly several years before "A Rose for Emily," which it so strikingly resembles.[6] Miss Gant is described as having dreams that seem to come straight out of a Freudian case study:

She would wake from dreams in which the painter performed monstrously with his pot and brush. In the dream his eyes were yellow instead of gray, and he was always chewing, his chin fading away into the blurred drool of the chewing; one night she waked herself by saying aloud, "He's got a beard!" Now and then she dreamed of the pot and brush alone. They would be alive, performing of themselves actions of monstrous and ritualistic significance.

In "A Rose for Emily" perversion and decadence are a subtle effluvium from the story, from the town's nostalgia, Miss Emily's peculiar relation to past generations, the severity of her father and her warped affection for him. Miss Emily becomes a part of, or better, becomes the mystery itself — "like a carven torso of an idol in a niche, looking, looking or not looking at us, we could never tell which. Thus she passed from generation to generation — dear, inescapable, impervious, tranquil, and perverse." The reader's shock upon learning that she had killed her lover and lain beside him year after year owes much of its quality to the subtlety with which Faulkner has presented her. In *Miss Zilphia Gant* the young writer had so stressed and underscored the strangeness of his situation that it becomes difficult to assent to its reality. Reading the two stories one after the other makes it abundantly clear that Faulkner had, in a surprisingly short time, learned how to "perform something bold and tragical and austere."

A Part of the
Southern Mores: Protestantism

BY THE TIME OF the publication of *Light in August*, in October 1932, the critics were aware of Faulkner as a writer about whom one had to hold a strong, if not a reasoned, opinion. Geoffrey Stone in the *Bookman* said the novel was "like an epileptic fit. . . . Despite his great gifts and deep sensitivity, what he is actually offering us is a flight from reality. His horrors and obscenities in no way contradict this, for many persons, tired of ordinary life, have been known to seek amusement courting nightmares." Dorothy Van Doren found him no Dostoyevsky because his works lack "passionate ratiocination. The activities of Faulkner's characters, when the reader is made aware of them at all, take place almost entirely in the viscera." Few or none of the reviewers recognized that this novel at center is a probing into the terrible excesses of the Calvinist spirit.*

If one does not perceive that the Calvinist spirit is the central

NOTE: This chapter is reprinted, with modifications, from the original version in the *Hopkins Review*, vol. 5, no. 3 (Spring 1952), by permission of the editor. The essay has also appeared in Louis D. Rubin, Jr., and Robert D. Jacobs (eds.), *Southern Renascence: The Literature of the Modern South* (Johns Hopkins Press, 1953).

* It has been suggested that the novel is two separate stories, the Lena Grove–Byron Bunch story and the Joe Christmas–Joanna Burden–Hightower–Jefferson story. This probably is not so. There are three strands in the novel: (1) Lena Grove–Byron Bunch, (2) Hightower, and (3) Joe Christmas, all of which relate to the theme of rigidity of spirit as opposed to the need for

issue in *Light in August,* the novel will of necessity seem confused in theme. The Civil War and the black shadow of slavery, as some critics insist, suffuse the novel. It is proper enough to relive with Hightower the imagined scenes of galloping horses, burning buildings, the wounded and the dead of the Civil War; these do live on into the 1920s, even in the minds of those less crippled by such memories than the defrocked old minister. But the greater force, in which the War and the black shadow are caught up, is Calvinism, and, larger than it, rigidity of principle and harshness of spirit; and it is this force that menaces Joe Christmas, the putative Negro, and that persecutes Hightower. Byron Bunch and Lena Grove are more than comic relief; they are proof that one need not succumb to such a force.

The irony of the name Joe Christmas is noted by every reader of *Light in August.* (And it is equally obvious that other names in the novel have their appropriateness also: Gail Hightower, Percy Grimm, Calvin Burden, Bobbie [Barbara] Allen, Lena Grove, Byron Bunch, and Euphues Hines.) Certainly the major significance in the name is the irony of Joe Christmas' being pursued and harassed throughout his life by voices of Christian righteousness: Old Doc Hines, his mad grandfather, McEachern, his stern foster parent, and Joanna Burden, his guilt-haunted lover, and finally by

acceptance of human frailty and fallibility and the need for pity and sympathy.

Joe Christmas is also the victim of another kind of excess, the by-passing of deserved punishment. When as a five-year-old he steals and eats toothpaste, he expects to be punished, but the dietitian, who believes he has witnessed the intercourse between her and a young intern, tries to buy him off. Later Mrs. McEachern attempts to scheme with him to outwit the restrictions and rigidity of her husband, but young Christmas is more at ease with the excesses of McEachern than he is with the softness and weakness, as he sees it, of Mrs. McEachern. In other words, he wants to live inside a system of rules and sanctions. He associates softness and blind devotion with women and is contemptuous of them.

Hightower's relationship with Christmas is never made quite explicit, but there seems to be at least a hint of homosexuality in it.[1] However, in contrasting the sexuality of Christmas with that of Joanna Burden, the author comments that while she was terribly perverted Christmas was not: "Within six months she was completely corrupted. It could not be said he corrupted her. His own life, for all its anonymous promiscuity, had been conventional enough, as a life of healthy and normal sin usually is."

73

the society itself insofar as its religion, as Hightower claims, drives the community to *"crucifixion of themselves and one another."*

Euphues Hines is certain he is doing God's will in killing the man who had seduced his daughter, in refusing to allow a doctor to assist his daughter in the birth of her illegitimate son (after which she dies), in getting a job at the orphanage where he has secretly put the boy, then taking up a position as a threatening presence at the edge of the boy's consciousness, in allowing the boy to be adopted by Simon McEachern, and, twenty-five years later when Joe Christmas, now a murderer, is captured in Mottstown, in screaming that he should be lynched. Through it all runs the assurance that he, Hines, is God's instrument. One of his mad speeches is a bitter parody of the doctrine of predestination:

It was the Lord. *He* was there. Old Doc Hines give God His chance too. The Lord told old Doc Hines what to do and old Doc Hines done it. Then the Lord said to old Doc Hines, "You watch now. Watch My will a-working." And old Doc Hines watched and heard the mouths of little children, of God's own fatherless and motherless, putting His words and knowledge into their mouths even when they couldn't know it since they were without sin yet, even the girl ones without sin and bitchery yet: Nigger! Nigger! in the innocent mouths of little children. "What did I tell you?" God said to old Doc Hines. "And now I've set My will to working and now I'm gone. There aint enough sin here to keep Me busy because what do I care for the fornications of a slut, since that is a part of My purpose too," and old Doc Hines said, "How is the fornications of a slut a part of Your purpose too?" and God said, "You wait and see. Do you think it is just chanceso that I sent that young doctor to be the one that found My abomination laying wrapped in that blanket on that doorstep that Christmas night? Do you think it was just chanceso that the Madam should have been away that night and give them young sluts the chance and call to name him Christmas in sacrilege of My Son? So I am gone now, because I have set My will a-working and I can leave you to watch it."

Twenty years after the event Joe Christmas knew that the most lasting mark from his boyhood had been made the Sunday McEachern whipped him for failing to learn his Presbyterian catechism. The punishment had been given in all righteousness.

A Part of the Southern Mores: Protestantism

McEachern's "voice was not unkind. It was not human, personal, at all. It was just cold, implacable, like written or printed words." Several times, always after the passage of a full hour, the boy was whipped again. McEachern sat stiffly watching the boy, "one hand on his knee and the silver watch in the other palm, his clean, bearded face as firm as carved stone, his eyes ruthless, cold, but not unkind." Later the man knelt with the boy to ask "that Almighty be as magnanimous as himself" in forgiving the boy's disobedience. That day Christmas learned silent resistance.

And that evening, in refusing food brought by Mrs. McEachern —dumping the dishes on the floor—he learned how to refuse sympathy, to harden himself against the feminine world. He felt she was trying to make him cry. "Then she thinks they would have had me."

Joe Christmas was almost eighteen before he learned how to outwit McEachern in his niggardly denials of the flesh. A waitress, Bobbie Allen, also a semi-professional whore, is the first person from whom he accepts any sympathy, and he does this at first because of sexual desire for her. But McEachern destroys this relationship by following them to a country dance, where, like the "representative of a wrathful and retributive Throne," he calls her "harlot" and "Jezebel." Joe strikes him down with a chair and after stealing a small amount of money from Mrs. McEachern runs away. But Bobbie Allen is offended at the treatment she has had (Faulkner makes high comedy of her indignation at being called "harlot"), screams at him that he is a nigger, and allows her friends to beat him up.

The climactic parts of Joe Christmas' life are lived in Jefferson, where he becomes the lover of Joanna Burden, the spinster descendant of an abolitionist family from New Hampshire. The family had been Unitarians with the "agonized conscience" described by George Santayana in the well-known passage in his "Genteel Traditions in American Philosophy." They believed

that sin exists, that sin is punished, and that it is beautiful that sin should exist to be punished. The heart of Calvinism is therefore divided between tragic concern at its own miserable condition, and tragic exultation about the universe at large. . . . Human nature, it feels, is totally depraved: to have the instincts and motives that we necessarily have is a great scandal, and we must suffer for it; but that scandal is requisite, since otherwise the serious importance of being as we ought to be would not have been vindicated.

Joanna's grandfather and brother had been killed in Jefferson by Colonel Sartoris for "stirring up the Negroes." And she had heard such insistently held opinions as this of her grandfather's: "He got off on Lincoln and slavery and dared any man there to deny that Lincoln and the Negro and Moses and the children of Israel were the same, and that the Red Sea was just the blood that had to be spilled in order that the black race might cross into the Promised Land."

In conversations with Joe Christmas she rehearses the actions and long-held opinions in her family that establish their being outside the Latin desire to be at ease with the world. (In fact, there are passages in her story of the family history curiously similar to those in *Absalom, Absalom!* in which the two worlds, Protestant Mississippi and Catholic New Orleans are contrasted.) Joe Christmas knows that Joanna's helping the Negro is a duty undertaken, but that it is abstract and impersonal. She acts not out of sympathy for other human beings but out of an obligation to carry out God's design in a depraved world. It is a helpless world, and the Negro's plight finally is irremediable. Her father tells her: "You must struggle, rise. But in order to rise, you must raise the shadow with you. . . . You can never lift it to your level." The suffering of the Negro *and* the guilt over slavery are the outward signs of a terribly guilt-ridden world — and both are permanent.

Joe Christmas believes that the demonic quality of Joanna's sexual perversions are the excesses inevitable to one who believes in the New England biblical hell and who feeds her emotion-starved body in spite of it. Faulkner describes Joanna's corruption as it appears to Joe Christmas:

At first it shocked him: the abject fury of the New England glacier exposed suddenly to the fire of the New England biblical hell. Perhaps he was aware of the abnegation in it: the imperious and fierce urgency that concealed an actual despair at frustrate and irrevocable years, which she appeared to attempt to compensate each night as if she believed that it would be the last night on earth by damning herself forever to the hell of her forefathers, by living not alone in sin but in filth. She had an avidity for the forbidden word symbols; an insatiable appetite for the sound of them on his tongue and on her own. She revealed the terrible and impersonal curiosity of a child about forbidden subjects and objects; that rapt and tireless and detached interest of a surgeon in the physical body and its possibilities. And by day he would see the calm, coldfaced, almost manlike, almost middleaged woman who had lived for twenty years alone, without any feminine fears at all, in a lonely house in a neighborhood populated, when at all, by Negroes, who spent a certain portion of each day sitting tranquilly at a desk and writing tranquilly for the eyes of both youth and age the practical advice of a combined priest and banker and trained nurse.

Driven mad by a sense of lost youth and her fear of damnation, she none the less holds unquestioningly to her own beliefs. Like Euphues Hines she sees herself as God's instrument — declares that it is God, not she, insisting that Joe Christmas pray:

They looked at one another. "Joe," she said, "for the last time. I don't ask it. Remember that. Kneel with me."

"No," he said. Then he saw her arms unfold and her right hand come forth from beneath the shawl. It held an old style, single action, cap-and-ball revolver almost as long and heavier than a small rifle. But the shadow of it and of her arm and hand on the wall did not waver at all, the shadow of both monstrous, the cocked hammer monstrous, back-hooked and viciously poised like the arched head of a snake; it did not waver at all. And her eyes did not waver at all. They were as still as the round black ring of the pistol muzzle. But there was no heat in them, no fury. They were calm and still as all pity and all despair and all conviction. But he was not watching them. He was watching the shadowed pistol on the wall; he was watching when the cocked shadow of the hammer flicked away.

The pistol misfired. Then he killed her, almost severing the head from her body.

Following the murder, Christmas is hunted and finally caught. During the days he is a fugitive he is involved in a number of violent acts, but one in particular is appropriate to the theme the novel is dramatizing. It is the scene, reported by a member of the Negro congregation, in which Christmas breaks up a revival meeting:

He [the member of the congregation] had come direct from a Negro church twenty miles away, where a revival meeting was in nightly progress. On the evening before, in the middle of a hymn, there had come a tremendous noise from the rear of the church, and turning the congregation saw a man standing in the door. The door had not been locked or even shut yet the man had apparently grasped it by the knob and hurled it back into the wall so that the sound crashed into the blended voices like a pistol shot. . . . a woman began to shriek . . . "It's the devil! It's Satan himself." Then she ran, quite blind. She ran straight toward him and he knocked her down without stopping and stepped over her and went on, with the faces gaped for screaming falling away before him, straight to the pulpit and put his hand on the minister. . . . "We could see Brother Bedenberry talking with him, trying to pacify him quiet, and him jerking at Brother Bedenberry and slapping his face with his hand. . . . And he began to curse, hollering it out, at the folks, and he cursed God louder than the women screeching . . ."

It is as though Christmas knows, and perhaps we are to infer that he does know, that the church, far from making his life easier, is one of the agents of his destruction.

The tragedy of Hightower is presented less directly than that of Christmas, mostly as remembered experiences. Hightower's speculations upon his own history and the character of Jefferson furnish most of the explicit commentary on the significance of the action. We learn that he was born to middle-aged parents, an invalid mother and a fifty-year-old father, a minister and doctor, who though strongly opposed to slavery served four years in the Confederate Army. A point is made about the father's character by stating that he would neither eat the food nor sleep in a bed prepared by a Negro.

Hence during the War and while he was absent from home, his

A Part of the Southern Mores: Protestantism

wife had no garden save what she could make herself or with the infrequent aid of neighbors. And this aid the husband would not allow her to accept for the reason that it could not be repaid in kind. "God will provide," he said.

"Provide what? Dandelions and ditch weeds?"

"Then He will give us the bowels to digest them."

Hightower was born after the War, inheriting organs which "required the unflagging care of a Swiss watch." As a child he was fascinated, bewitched by the War and lived with "those phantoms who loomed heroic and tremendous against a background of thunder and smoke and torn flags." Thinking of it caused him to "experience a kind of hushed and triumphant terror which left him a little sick."

Hightower's grandfather, a gruff man who smelled of whisky and cigars, had greeted his son's bride with this observation: "'I reckon you'll do,' he said. His eyes were bluff and bold, but kind. 'All the sanctimonious cuss wants anyway is somebody that can sing alto out of a Presbyterian hymnbook, where even the good Lord himself could not squeeze any music.'" One of the grandfather's amusements was to turn church revivals held in a grove into "a week of amateur horse racing while to a dwindling congregation gaunt, fanaticfaced country preachers thundered anathema from the rustic pulpit at his oblivious and unregenerate head." The grandfather had been killed in "Van Dorn's cavalry raid to destroy Grant's stores in Jefferson." This too was one of young Hightower's torturing phantoms, causing him shudderings of delight. His own father, although alive, was also a kind of phantom to the boy. He and his invalid mother looked upon the father as foreign to them, almost an intruder. Hightower lived in a twilight vision of a cavalry troop galloping into Jefferson.

In the seminary, to which he was drawn by its promise of peace, he told himself repeatedly, "God must call me to Jefferson because my life died there, was shot from the saddle of a galloping horse in a Jefferson street one night twenty years before it was ever born." That the seminary had not proved to be the sanctuary

79

for the "garment-worried spirit" he had hoped for did not trouble Hightower greatly because it was merely a preparation for his getting to Jefferson. In the seminary he met his wife. She was the daughter of one of the ministers who was a member of the faculty. Hightower did not live in the everyday world and did not know that she could live there all her life and not be beautiful, nor did he know that for "three years her eyes had watched him with almost desperate calculation, like those of a harassed gambler." Once she spoke suddenly of marriage and escape:

"Escape?" he said. "Escape from what?"
"This!" she said. He saw her face for the first time as a living face, as a mask before desire and hatred; wrung blind, headlong with passion. Not stupid: just blind, reckless, desperate. "All of it! All! All!"

Hightower's congregation in Jefferson had thought him a little mad when from the pulpit in his rapt, eager voice he preached of God, salvation, his grandfather, and galloping horses. Looking back at his life, Hightower said he had failed his congregation because he had not preached to them of mercy, pity, and the forgiveness of human frailty. He knew too that he had failed his wife. Eventually she had scandalized Jefferson by not attending church, going away suspiciously for weekends, once screaming at her husband during his sermon, and finally jumping from a hotel room in Memphis where she had been registered under a fictitious name as someone else's wife. Hightower had refused to resign and for a time, before the parishioners locked him out, he had preached and prayed in an empty church. The congregation wanted him to leave Jefferson and gave him a sum of money, but he refused to leave and settled on a little side street. He remained even after he had been taken out of town by the Ku Klux Klan, tied to a tree, and beaten unconscious.

The last trial Hightower is subjected to is a request from Byron Bunch (who is scheming for his own purposes) and Christmas' grandmother, Mrs. Hines, for him to swear that Christmas could not have killed Miss Burden because he had spent the night of the murder and many other nights with Hightower. The old minister

A Part of the Southern Mores: Protestantism

refuses to suffer this last outrage, but when Percy Grimm pursues Christmas into Hightower's house he does try to prevent the murder by declaring that Christmas had spent that night with him.

Because Hightower, despite his many weaknesses, was capable of nobility of motive and action, his view of the church, stated shortly before his death, must be stressed:

> It seems to him that he has seen it all the while: that that which is destroying the Church is not the outward groping of those within it nor the inward groping of those without, but the professionals who control it and who have removed the bells from its steeples. He seems to see them, endless, without order, empty, symbolical, bleak, skypointed not with ecstasy or passion but in adjuration, threat, and doom. He seems to see the churches of the world like a rampart, like one of those barricades of the middleages planted with dead and sharpened stakes, against truth and against that peace in which to sin and be forgiven which is the life of man.

Earlier in the story Hightower had singled out one service, that on Sunday evening, as the only one during which "there is something of that peace which is the promise and end of the church." It is an hour of faith and hope. Hightower looks forward to this hour in the week when from his darkened window he will watch the people move toward the church. On Sunday nights during the summer he loves to listen to the organ tones, rich and resonant. But on the Sunday before the lynching of Joe Christmas he thinks:

> Yet even then the music has still a quality stern and implacable, deliberate and without passion so much as immolation, pleading, asking, for not love, not life, forbidding it to others, demanding in sonorous tones death, as though death were the boon, like all Protestant music. . . . Listening to it he seems to hear within it the apotheosis of his own history, his own land, his own environed blood: Pleasure, ecstasy they cannot seem to bear. Their escape from it is in violence, in drinking and fighting and praying; catastrophe too, the violence identical and apparently inescapable. *And so why should not their religion drive them to crucifixion of themselves and one another?*

Of the lynching, he says:

> And they will do it gladly, gladly. . . . Since to pity him would be to admit self-doubt and to hope for and need pity themselves.

They will do it gladly, gladly. That's what is so terrible, terrible.

Hightower was right about how it would be done. Percy Grimm, another of the avatars of self-righteousness, is the town's instrument in the killing of Joe Christmas. He does not act in the name of deity, but he moves with the same aura of assured virtue. He sees himself the agent of pure patriotism — which in the context means the protection of each detail of the mores, whatever its source. Faulkner insists on the righteousness of Grimm: "There was nothing vengeful about him either, no fury, no outrage" as he pursued Joe Christmas across ditches, behind cabins, and finally into Hightower's house. And the righteousness is further insisted upon in the description of his voice when Hightower, lying to prevent the lynching, says Christmas had spent the night of the murder with him: "'Jesus Christ,' Grimm cried, his young voice clear and outraged like that of a young priest." Then the outrage turns into an insane kind of fury (like that of Hines or Joanna Burden) and Grimm castrates Joe Christmas with a butcher knife.

Lena Grove and Byron Bunch are not merely the comic subplot, the relief from the terrible anguish of the lynching. They are a part of the complexity of the community, and by what they are and the way they act they insinuate powerfully what is wrong with the community. Only rarely does Faulkner allow them to comment explicitly on the other part of the action, as when Lena Grove sees in Hightower's face "that ruthlessness which she had seen in the face of a few good people, usually men." Neither she nor Byron Bunch is the intelligent refractor, in Henry James' terms, of the action; it is by being what they are that they imply a commentary.*

Lena is a creature of faith, humility, and endurance. Setting out from Alabama in her eighth month of pregnancy and with only thirty-five cents, she hopefully expects to find her seducer. In her trustfulness and willingness to be helped, she accepts the attentions and

---

* It is quite possible that Faulkner took from Shakespeare, or from his knowledge of Elizabethan drama, which he is said to know quite well, his use of episodic structure and free intermingling of characters from different levels. This structure undoubtedly contributes to the sense of multiple life that many of his stories give.

assistance of many, including Bunch. Her manner causes the people she meets, or most of them, to treat her in kind, generously, courteously. But she is not without guile. She knows how to lead Byron about, taking an almost but not quite innocent advantage of his abject devotion. She belongs among those who are fallible but who live in "tranquil obedience . . . to the good earth." She is a minor earth goddess. Harshness of spirit and rigidity of principle are completely foreign to her.

Burch, the seducer of Lena, is characterless. He stands outside the two groups that dominate the novel, those with the religious beliefs that cause them to crucify their fellowman and those, like Lena and Byron, with the kind of belief that makes existence sufferable and even pleasant. He is a kind of Judas (and is called just that) in his willingness to sacrifice his friend Joe Christmas, but actually he is amoral and therefore hardly human at all. Byron says Burch "was just living on the country, like a locust." He has no pride in himself and he has no sense of responsibility. He is capable neither of loyalty nor love.

Byron Bunch, on the other hand, has committed himself to the moral life, to a Protestant orthodoxy. He is the friend of Hightower (who offers him the conventionally good man's advice to avoid Lena), and he is a choir leader. Obviously a product of the Protestant ethic, he is described as having "a still stubborn, ascetic face: the face of a hermit who has lived for a long time in an empty place where the sand blows." He believes in the sanctity of work, that a man gets into mischief when he is not working; therefore he works on Saturday afternoons and keeps a record of the hours he is not working. He attempts to search out the truth and he worries his conscience, but he is never self-righteous. Except that he has humor about himself, he belongs to the tradition of Piers Plowman and of Bunyan's Christian, a kind of Protestant Everyman. Faulkner identifies him as belonging to the hill people, the pine hill farmers, and describes him as "small, non-descript, whom no man ever turned to look at twice." He is the only significant character whose background is not explored.

But Byron is free from the excesses of the Protestant tradition.

The Tangled Fire of William Faulkner

He is not in search of martyrdom, but he endures the hardships that his sense of obligation tells him are his to accept. He can admit self-doubt, he can pity, and he is charitable. Faulkner describes him as acting kindly "as a reflex." He is fallible and, like Lena, capable of guile, but Byron Bunch believes in "that peace," as Hightower describes it, which results from sinning and being forgiven, "which is the life of man."

That *Light in August* is not a sociological document is clear enough. The whole manner of its telling cries out that it is highly stylized — the complex and subtle patterns of imagery, the frequently exaggerated situations, the furiously mad or idyllically sane characters, the paralleling of details from the life of Christ until the death of Christmas seems a monstrous and grotesque irony, and so on. The variety of characters, the interplay of carefully selected episodes, as well as the furiously sustained and sometimes facile flow of language, establish the greatness of the novel as a work of art.

As in *The Sound and the Fury* one sees Faulkner writing both in and out of the tradition passed on to him by Conrad, James, and Joyce. Unlike Joyce, who desired to refine the author out of existence, to have him sit godlike above his created work, Faulkner frequently has insisted upon writing in his own voice. The following passages from *Light in August*, arranged in an ascending order, suggest how he moves from style-as-subject to style-as-his-own-voice. In the first passage Joe Christmas, semiconscious after a severe beating, hears a voice above him talking about the money Christmas has tried to give to Bobbie Allen, the waitress and prostitute with whom he has been in love:

Here bobbie here kid heres your comb you forgot it heres romeos chicken feed too jesus he must have tapped the sunday school till on the way out its bobbies now didnt you see him give it to her didnt you see old bighearted thats right pick it up kid you can keep it as an installment or a souvenir or something what dont she want it well say thats too bad.

In the second passage the fifteen years of Joe Christmas' wandering is caught in an image of one street turning into the towns and cities in which he has pursued and been pursued by his obsession:

> The whiskey died away in time and was renewed and died again, but the street ran on. From that night the thousand streets ran as one street, with imperceptible corners and changes of scene, broken by intervals of begged and stolen rides, on trains and trucks, and on country wagons with which he at twenty and twentyfive and thirty sitting on the seat with his still, hard face and the clothes (even when soiled and worn) of a city man and the driver of the wagon not knowing who or what the passenger was and not daring to ask. The street ran into Oklahoma and Missouri. . . . It was fifteen years long: it ran between savage and spurious board fronts of oil towns where, his inevitable serge clothing and light shoes black with bottomless mud, he ate crude food. . . . It ran through yellow wheat fields waving beneath the cold mad moon of September, and the brittle stars. . . . And always, sooner or later, the street ran through an identical and well-nigh interchangeable section of cities without remembered names, where beneath the dark and equivocal and symbolical archways of midnight he bedded with the women, and paid them when he had money, and when he did not have it he bedded anyway and then told them he was a Negro.

In the third passage the consciousness of Joe Christmas as a child is used as a basis for generalizing about the way character and belief and conviction are formed prior to or aside from conscious knowledge:

> Memory believes before knowing remembers. Believes longer than recollects, longer than knowing even wonders. Knows remembers believes a corridor in a big long garbled cold echoing building of dark red brick soot-blackened by more chimneys than its own, set in a grassless cinderstrewnpacked compound surrounded by smoking factory purlieus and enclosed by a ten foot steel-and-wire fence like a penitentiary or a zoo, where in random erratic surges, with sparrowlike, childtrebling orphans in identical and uniform blue denim in and out of remembering but in knowing constant as the bleak walls, the bleak windows where in rain soot from the yearly adjacenting chimneys streaked like black tears.

The experience is the child's, but the language is unmistakably Faulkner's own.

The Tangled Fire of William Faulkner

Common to all of these passages, and to his whole method, is Faulkner's attempt to draw the reader into the story. To this end he is willing, when necessary, to ignore the orthodoxies of expository prose and — in his own voice — to brave the currents and eddies of a poetic idiom. In the third of the passages quoted there are the phrases "black tears," "childtrebling," and "garbled cold echoing building," all examples of Faulkner's willingness to coin terms or to force new connotations.

Light in August might also be examined in terms of the psychology of sex, especially in relation to the social or racial situation treated in it. Probably it is remaining closer to the main intention of the novel, however, to see it in terms of the Protestant mores, a subject with which Faulkner seems preoccupied. Certainly it is mark of his genius that Faulkner can develop the terrible irony that it is out of the religion itself that the lynching comes, without resting in it, and is able to introduce the complementary theme, that inside the religion one can also find direction, discipline, and consolation.

Once having recognized that Faulkner is concerned with the spirit of Protestantism in the southern mores, one is surprised at the frequency with which he examines it. Righteous Baptist ladies are satirized in *Sanctuary*, Preacher Whitfield in *As I Lay Dying* is one of the most despicable figures in the Faulkner canon, and Cora Tull in the same novel is close to being the essence of simpleminded self-satisfaction. The Sartorises in *The Unvanquished* are described as living in a land produced by a merging of "violent sun, of violent alternation from snow to heat-stroke" with "mistborn Protestantism." The landlord doctor and his wife in *The Wild Palms* act partly out of a sense of decency but also out of vindictive righteousness and "grim Samaritan husbandry." Protestantism in *Absalom, Absalom!* is presented as stern, inflexible, and lacking in charity; and as late as *Intruder in the Dust* we find a description like this: "he remembered the tall spires which said Peace and the squatter utilitarian belfries which said Repent and he remembered one which even said Beware but this one said simply: Burn." There is even a humorous treatment of such grim righteousness in one of the short stories, "Uncle Willy." [2]

A Part of the Southern Mores: Protestantism

The story of Uncle Willy, narrated by a fourteen-year-old boy, is centered in the effort of sanctimonious church women to cure the likable and orderly but ineffectual old druggist of his forty-year habit of taking dope:

But they made him quit. It didn't take them long. It began one Sunday morning and it was finished by the next Friday; we had just sat down in our class and Mr. Barbour had just begun, when all of a sudden Reverend Schultz, the minister, was there, leaning over Uncle Willy and already hauling him out of his seat when we looked around, hauling him up and saying in that tone in which preachers speak to fourteen-year-old boys that I don't believe even pansy boys like . . . and Reverend Schultz shoving him into Mrs. Merridew's car and Mrs. Merridew saying, loud, like she was in the pulpit: "Now, Mr. Christian, I'm going to fix you a nice glass of cool lemonade and then we will have a nice chicken dinner and then you are going to take a nice nap in my hammock and then Brother and Sister Schultz are coming out and we will have some nice ice cream," and Uncle Willy saying, "No. Wait, ma'am, wait! Wait! I got to go to the store and fill a prescription I promised this morning."

Faulkner's sympathies are obviously with Uncle Willy, not with the righteous church people. One has little difficulty accepting the report from Oxford that at the time Faulkner was scoutmaster "hard shell Baptist opinion considered him unfit for the post."

The Folklore of Speed

A GREEN BOUGH, Faulkner's second volume of verse, was published in 1933. Reviewers were not much impressed with it, noting that Faulkner had only imperfectly assimilated his influences. They agreed that, unlike the complex structure of the novels, the substance of the poems was hardly more than a fragrance, or a slight shadow of words. Seemingly, he had written little verse since the New Orleans days, and the criticism he voiced to Phil Stone about the poems which had appeared in *The Marble Faun* [1] still applied to those in *A Green Bough:* [2] "his personal trouble as a poet seemed to be that he had one eye on the ball and the other eye on Babe Ruth."

Nor did *Dr. Martino,* [3] his second volume of short stories, fare particularly well with the reviewers, although William Rose Benét found it further proof, for him, of Faulkner's genius; "In the more compact medium he is doing some of the most powerful and original work that America can claim in our time." *

* About this time Faulkner did another stint in Hollywood, working with Nunnally Johnson and Howard Hawks on *The Road to Glory.* Johnson says Faulkner was hired to write "emotional scenes. It was Faulkner's strange emotional drama, or something of it, that we wanted in *The Road to Glory.* . . . He confined himself to specific scenes, leaving it to us to put in the technical directions. As he wrote them these scenes were always much too long, but editing them was a simple and pleasant matter, for they were always doubly dramatic when reduced to the compact form necessary for

The Folklore of Speed

A number of the stories in *Dr. Martino* show how deeply Faulkner by this time was involved in the materials of Yoknapatawpha County. "The Hound," centering on a "poor white" named Cotten, would later be developed in *The Hamlet*, but with Cotten becoming Mink Snopes. "There Was a Queen" is, as noted earlier, a further development of an episode from *Sartoris*, a satiric treatment of Narcissa Benbow's willingness to sacrifice her honor for her reputation. "A Mountain Victory," a Civil War story, concerns the death of Saucier Weddel, who has Choctaw and French blood. One might guess that if the Ikkemotube saga ever reaches the form of a novel this story will find a place in it.[4]

"Wash," told by a crisscrossing of events and moving backward and forward in time, is the germ of *Absalom, Absalom!* Diminished though it is by the subsequent novel, "Wash" remains a masterly piece of compression, the action seeming to move inside locally accepted notions of caste but suddenly whipping about, a peripety that destroys Sutpen and elevates Wash Jones to a position of great dignity.

A much less skillful story is "Smoke," set in Yoknopatawpha, which later became a part of *Knight's Gambit*. It is the first of the detective stories centering in the knowledgeable Gavin Stevens. Of the two war stories only "Turn About," the one made into the movie *Today We Live,* is very successful, and then only as adventure.

Several of the remaining stories, including the title story, "Dr. Martino," lack a strong commitment to theme and seem, despite brilliant touches, a little thin and poorly conceived. This is not true of the two stories, "Death Drag" and "Honor," which forecast Faulkner's next novel, *Pylon.*[5] The former has a grotesque and pathetic figure in Ginsfarb, the bankrupt merchant, who hates stunt flying with almost a demoniac hatred. His anger and grim determination about what he will and will not do are so intense that the very solidity of the earth and the laws of physics seem to

the movies." Faulkner worked conscientiously at his assignments, but obviously, and unlike, say, Scott Fitzgerald, he did not look upon himself as a professional script writer. And he always returned to Oxford as soon as possible.

give way before him. Presumably he is intended to be a symbol of man frustrated almost beyond endurance but able finally, out of his very willfulness, to win a thin margin of victory. "Honor," a story of two fliers loving the same woman, obviously is a source of *Pylon,* but it is much more conventional in conception than the novel.

In the *Wilson Library Bulletin* for June 1935 there is, accompanying the announcement that Faulkner's next book would be *Pylon,* a picture of William standing beside his plane at the Memphis airport. Two of his brothers were also pilots. John, the third brother, had taken up flying some years before, working as a duster of boll weevils in Georgia until he crashed his plane.[6] Dean, the youngest brother, barnstormed in William's plane. Within a few months after the publication of *Pylon* Dean crashed and was killed. Thereafter Faulkner did little flying, and that only for traveling purposes.

Pylon begins *in medias res.* The immediate action, taking place during the five days of a carnival in New Valois, or New Orleans, is concerned with the involvement in the air meet of a strange "family" of racing and stunt fliers and the violent death of one of them. They are seen in relationship with a young reporter who is a grotesque caricature of ineffectuality. The action pulls two ways, into the earlier lives of the "family" and into the disordered, bewildered life of the sentimental reporter.

The earlier lives of the "family" — made up of Roger Shumann, Laverne, and Jack, the parachute jumper — are sketched in flash backs, as in the conversations between Jiggs, their mechanic, and the reporter. Shumann, the son of a midwestern country doctor, has dedicated himself to putting machines together instead of preparing himself to be a doctor. As a member of a flying circus, he meets Laverne, whose life in the home of her sister has been sordid and depressing. Living with Shumann, Laverne later falls in love with Jack and takes to sleeping with both men, impartially dividing her affections. When a baby is to be born, the two men roll dice to decide which will officially become Laverne's husband. She marries Shumann. The "family" continue their earlier ways, the men alternating in going to bed with Laverne. Their lives are a series of cheap meals, dismal rooms, economic upsets, and the mad strain of aviation meets. In New Valois, during their sixth year together, Laverne is expecting another child. To get money for her confinement, Shumann flies dangerously close to the pylons, winning a second prize but finally crashing his plane. With the help of the reporter, who is infatuated with Laverne, he gets another plane, which the authorities allow him to fly although they know it could not pass inspection; Shumann is killed when it crashes into Lake Pontchartrain. The child is sent to the elderly Doctor Shumann, and Jack and Laverne continue their exacerbated lives, moving from air meet to air meet.

In a review of *Test Pilot*, by Jimmy Collins,[7] Faulkner made fairly explicit what he was probably trying, with small success, to do in *Pylon*:

I had hoped to find a kind of embryo, a still formless forerunner or symptom of a folklore of speed, the high speed of today which I believe stands a good deal nearer to the end of the limit which human beings and material were capable of when men first dug iron, than to the beginning of those limits as they stood ten or twelve years ago when men first began to go really fast. . . . Perhaps they will continue to create a kind of species or race, as they used to create and nurture races of singers and eunuchs. . . . But it was not of this folklore I was thinking . . . [but] of the speed itself.

Even in the review, he seems unable to bring his theme into clear focus. Faulkner felt confronted by a race of mortals who have or would soon cut themselves off from other human beings, be transformed in their dedication to the mechanics of speed. The years since he wrote the review have served to make such speculations seem a little fanciful and dated.

Presumably the reporter in *Pylon*, who is referred to as a J. Alfred Prufrock, is a representative of the old order, neither cautious nor politic certainly but obtuse, deferential, and glad to be of use. He belongs to T. S. Eliot's wasteland dramatis personae. He sees the urban world as even harsher than Eliot's character sees it, smells of cooking, sawdust restaurants, and men in shirt sleeves leaning out of windows. He sees it as screaming headlines, mad speed, and close to a dehumanized existence with creatures who will soon be "incapable of suffering, wombed and born complete and instantaneous, cunning and intricate and deadly, from out some blind iron batcave of the earth's prime foundation." The setting is a "wasteland" world, but the parallels with Prufrock are not many.

The intention of the story, one assumes, is to translate the frenzy of the "family's" lives in relation to flying into a frenzy of excitement over their lives as creatures of a new order. Presumably the reporter is the sexless impotent of Faulkner's literary generation. He is a "scarecrow in a winter field," "a dandelion burr," "a paper sack," and a prostitute says that taking money from him would be like assessing the spirit invoked at a seance. Yet even he is aroused by Laverne, whose sexuality seems transmuted from the speed and roar of the planes themselves. There is a scene in which she makes violent love to Shumann in a plane, then leaps to the fair grounds below, like a fleshly image of sex descending by parachute, arousing the passions of the whole community.

If the rush of Faulkner's rhetoric and the distraction of seeing the "family" as they drive the distraught reporter from anguished scene to anguished scene did not interfere, the situations might seem unintentionally funny. One does not give full credence to the reporter as a character, because he seems a literary convention, an *avant-garde* creation as opposed to his boss, the newspaper editor, who is a movie stereotype. In the "family" we believe, however much we may be interested in studying what they represent, only as we believe in the porcelain grimaces and writhing antics of puppets in skillful hands. The reader feels what Faulkner said he felt in finishing *Test Pilot*: "I was disappointed in this book. . . . I had expected, hoped, that it would be a kind of new trend, a literature or blundering at self expression, not of a man, but of this whole new business of speed just to be moving fast."

Pylon also invites one to question the wholehearted antimodernity which is usually attributed to Faulkner. Laverne and Shumann and Jack are as heroic as creatures half-human and half-metallic can be. They live within their own morbid, even masochistic idealism. Perhaps, however, something like this is closer to Faulkner's attitude: One is asked, not to like such characters, but to give them a little margin of admiration for having come to terms with a mechanized order, finding a part of their very being in it. If this is so, one would like to be able to see a little more deeply into the forces motivating them, to understand, if we may borrow a term from physics, the dialectric leap from machine to human spirit. That we don't understand it is the chief fault of *Pylon.*

Consequences of the Old Order

IN ABSALOM, ABSALOM!, published in
1936, Faulkner greatly deepens and extends the story of Thomas
Sutpen, which he had outlined in "Wash." Quentin Compson, a
young man at Harvard in 1909, imagines, talks out, and pieces
together the life of Sutpen, whose actions represent for him the
essence of the history of the South.* For Quentin the life of Sutpen
is a part of the mythos in which he himself still lives. "You can't
understand it. You would have to be born there," Quentin tells
his Canadian roommate Shreve McCannon.

Yet he does try to explain it, to tell the story of Thomas Sutpen
as the story of the South. He tells about the young mountain boy
who was turned from the front door of a great plantation house by
a livried Negro; how, chagrined and hurt, the boy dreamed of
owning such a house himself, with slaves and land and wealth;
how as a young man he appeared in Jefferson with twenty wild
slaves and an architect to build a plantation house on the property,

NOTE: This chapter is reprinted, with modifications, from the original version
in *Western Humanities Review*, vol. 7, no. 4 (Fall 1953), by permission of
the managing editor.

* Ward Miner suggests that Sutpen's career is based in rough outline on
the life of Alexander H. Pegues, a man who rose from poverty to affluence in
Oxford before the Civil War. This may be quite true, but it would be a
serious mistake not to stress the legendary and mythical quality that Sutpen,
the fictional character, takes on.[1]

one hundred square miles, bought from the Chickasaws; and how, a generation and many violent events later, Sutpen was killed, his "design," as he called it, come to nothing.

In his late years, Sutpen asks Quentin's grandfather: "Where did I make the mistake . . . what did I do or misdo . . . whom or what injure by it to the extent this would indicate? I had a design. To accomplish it I should require money, a house, a plantation, slaves, a family — incidentally of course, a wife. I set out to acquire these asking no favor of any man." Quentin attempts to understand Sutpen's life, the life which seems to him the legend of his own region's past.

Absalom, Absalom!, in part a story of miscegenation, is southern. But the ultimate point of the story is suggested by the title. Thomas Sutpen as a young man trying to make his fortune in the West Indies puts away his first wife and their son, Charles, because he discovers she has Negro blood. By a second marriage back in Mississippi, where he is attempting to establish a great plantation (Sutpen's Hundred), he has two children, Henry and Judith. Through the strategem of the first wife, Charles, his relationship still secret, enters into the lives of his half-brother and half-sister, becoming a close friend of Henry and the fiancé of Judith. Charles uses the engagement as a means of reaching his father, and he would be satisfied to leave Sutpen's Hundred forever if Thomas Sutpen would acknowledge him, give him some sign of affection or sympathy. But Sutpen refuses, and Charles, who then insists on marrying Judith, is killed by Henry.

Many lives, black and white, are destroyed by Sutpen's inability to acknowledge Charles, to break through the terrible taboo that separates black from white. The tragedy is southern, but it is more than that — it is the tragedy of the son whose father refuses him his proper and needed recognition and acceptance. In our modern idiom, it is called the search for a father.

Every reader of *Absalom, Absalom!* is stirred by the last lines of the novel. Shreve, at the very end of the Sutpen story, says:

"I want you to tell me just one thing more. Why do you hate the South?"

The Tangled Fire of William Faulkner

"I don't hate it," Quentin said quickly, at once, immediately: "I don't hate it," he said. *I don't hate it* he thought, panting in the cold air, the iron New England dark; *I don't. I don't! I don't hate it! I don't hate it!*

Quentin Compson's intensely troubled denial certainly is not defensive in the usual manner of being loyal to one's home. Fascination and loathing and love and respect are inextricably intermingled. Quentin, brooding, driven, obsessed and torn by his affections and honor, belongs to the land cursed by slavery, to its lives and conflicts and to the social order in which the curse is seen working out its expiation.

Thomas Sutpen has been dead forty years by the time Quentin tells his story. But Quentin knows it is his story as well as Sutpen's:

It was a day of listening too — the listening, the hearing in 1909 mostly about that which he already knew, since he had been born in and still breathed the same air in which the church bells had rung on that Sunday morning in 1833 and, on Sundays, heard even one of the original three bells in the same steeple where descendants of the same pigeons strutted and crooned or wheeled in short courses resembling soft fluid paint-smears on the soft summer sky.

Quentin's grandfather knew Sutpen well, so that Quentin had grown up knowing the Sutpen story. Because he is a Compson, Rosa Coldfield — to whom Sutpen had crudely proposed marriage after the death of his wife Ellen, Rosa's sister — asks him to accompany her to the old ramshackle house. There they find Henry Sutpen, returned home to die. Sometime later, when Rosa comes back to take Henry to a hospital, Quentin witnesses the burning of the house, set afire by Clytie, Thomas Sutpen's daughter by a Negro slave. Quentin also witnesses the death of Henry, the last of the Sutpens, except for Jim Bon, the idiot grandson of Charles Bon and his octaroon mistress or wife. As with the Compson family, an idiot is left, a gibbering commentary on the disintegration of an older order.

Quentin explains to Shreve how Thomas Sutpen, the former mountain boy, tried by sheer force of will to complete his design: struggling violently to build a position and estate to pass on to his family; fighting through four years of war and returning to Jefferson to find his wife dead, his son a fugitive, his property about to be seized for debts; hoping, as a man in his sixties, to found another family line on the body of Milly Jones, granddaughter of Wash Jones, his obsequious admirer, only to beget a daughter; then, in despair, provoking Jones into killing him.

The most puzzling part of *Absalom, Absalom!*, reminiscent of Quentin's preoccupation in *The Sound and the Fury,*[*] is Henry Sutpen's willingness to condone incest, his willingness to have Charles marry Judith — to have all of them, Thomas, Judith, Charles, and himself cast eternally into hell:

> It isn't yours nor his nor the Pope's hell [Henry says, addressing Charles] that we are going to: it's my mother's and her mother's and father's and their mother's and father's hell, and it isn't you who are going there, but we, the three — no: four of us. And so at least we will all be together where we belong, since even if only he went there we would still have to be there too since the three of us are just illusions that he begot, and your illusions are a part of you like your bones and flesh and memory. And we will all be together in torment and so we will not need to remember love and fornication, and maybe in torment you cannot remember why you are there. And if we cannot remember all this, it can't be much torment.

At this point, Henry knows Charles is his elder brother but he does not know Charles is partly Negro. Shortly after this, in the narrative, Henry talks with his father, Colonel Sutpen, telling him he is quite reconciled, even willing to have Charles marry Judith. The War is lost. Soon they will be home. God has quit their cause. He says to his father: "When you dont have God and honor and pride, nothing matters except that there is the old mindless meat that dont even care if it was defeat or victory, that wont even

---

[*] The perverse motives that drove Quentin to an early suicide ("waiting first to complete the current academic year and so get the full value of his paid-in-advance tuition") at Harvard in June 1910 are evident in Faulkner's notes on him in the genealogy of the Compsons, 1699–1945, furnished for *The Portable Faulkner*: ". . . who loved not the idea of incest which he would not commit, but some Presbyterian concept of its eternal punishment: he, not God, could by that means cast himself and his sister both into hell, where he could guard her forevermore amid the eternal fires."

die, that will be out in the woods and fields, grubbing up roots and weeds. — Yes. I have decided, Brother or not, I have decided. I will. I will."

The reader infers that this desire for incest must be an acceptance of defeat and, to use Faulkner's word, of doom. The people who have lived to themselves, who have set themselves up as a superior race, apart from the race over whom they have fought a civil war, have already committed spiritual incest.

Thomas Sutpen then tells Henry that Charles has Negro blood. Hitherto Henry has had no hint of it. He leaves his father and rejoins Charles, who can tell from his face and his manner what has happened. Charles says to Henry:

— So it's the miscegenation, not the incest, which you cant bear. Henry doesn't answer.
— And he sent me no word? He did not ask you to send me to him? That was all he had to do, now, today. . . . He didn't need to tell you I am a nigger to stop me. He could have stopped me without that, Henry.

When Charles insists that he will go through with the marriage, Henry replies that he cannot, that he will kill him to prevent it. Charles offers him a pistol, saying he should kill him now, or he will have to later. Henry takes the pistol but is unable to fire it. "You are my brother," he says, and throws it down. He breaks through a part of the taboo, acknowledging his brother. But he refuses to allow the marriage and at the gate of Sutpen's house he does shoot Charles. Then Wash Jones appears in town to say to Rosa Coldfield: "Henry has done shot that durn French feller. Kilt him dead as a beef."

Clearly, it is the taboo that black shall not marry white that kills Charles Bon. Clearly, too, Henry is not merely an individual, just as the possible incest is not merely a case of incest: Henry is southern white inability to accept the Negro as human equal. It is significant that these exchanges — the explanation of the Sutpen story — come very near the end of *Absalom, Absalom!*

On the final page of the novel one hears the voice of the ironic Shreve, who has helped Quentin understand the more than haunting story, say that in the end the Bons got rid of the Sutpens, that all but one of the warring families are dead — Jim, the idiot: "'You still hear him at night sometimes. Dont you?' 'Yes,' Quentin said." Shreve then says that the future will be with the Negro:

I think that in time the Jim Bonds [Bon has become Bond for the townspeople] are going to conquer the western hemisphere. Of course it won't quite be in our time and of course as they spread toward the poles they will bleach out again like rabbits and the birds do, so they won't show up against the snow. But it will still be Jim Bond; and so in a few thousand years, I who regard you will also have sprung from the loins of African kings.

The narrative structure of *Absalom, Absalom!*, which caused many reviewers a great deal of dissatisfaction and gave a few of them excuse for witty dismissal of the novel, is involved in its meaning.[2] The essence of the plot, the outline of the action, is given in the opening pages. But it is Quentin's story rather than the story of Thomas Sutpen, who died not understanding the meaning of the life that had been his. Quentin, with the aid of his father, Rosa Coldfield, and even Shreve McCannon, recreates the separate scenes, studies them, probes their significance. He sees the lives that Sutpen, in his terrible innocence, had destroyed — he sees Sutpen as a prototype of the southern white, not merely the slave owner, who sets his humanity above other humanity.

Faulkner tells the story, as he has told others, by moving backward and forward in time, from character to character, from scene to scene — until the reader is bewilderingly involved in an action he comprehends only in part. But what he does understand he experiences almost as a participant. And when the last sentence is read, and he can draw back for a look at the highly complex structure, he sees how intensely meaningful a given episode or scene, at first only vaguely comprehensible, has become in retrospect.

Absalom, Absalom! is sometimes called a Gothic novel — and it is, if one is free to use *Gothic* for a tale that is heavy with historical meanings. The mysteries, violence, and horror are present in abundance: the slaves following the bridal party carrying aloft the burning pine knots; the hunting of the fleeing architect with the dogs through the swamps; father and son and brother and brother talking in shadows on dim battlefields; brother shooting brother at the gate of the plantation; the decapitation of the chief protagonist, the "demon," with a scythe; the ruin of a once wealthy land; the roaring in flames of the great house; the slack-jawed idiot seeming to hover half disembodied in the night. . . . But the fictional horrors are there to dramatize in a terrible luminosity, with thunder, lightning, and alarms, a horror that not even the daylight of the year 1909, as far from Jefferson as Harvard College, has served to extinguish.

It was for *Absalom, Absalom!* that Faulkner first furnished his now famous map of Yoknapatawpha Co., Mississippi, William Faulkner, Sole Owner & Proprietor.* On the map one sees the fishing camp where Wash Jones killed Sutpen, Sutpen's plantation, Miss Rosa Coldfield's house on the road out from Jefferson, and so on. On the map, too, are appropriate markings for the Compsons, such as the designation of the pasture sold so Quentin could go to Harvard. Studying the map after reading *Absalom, Absalom!*, one may feel the rightness of Harvey Breit's observation that of all Faulkner's novels this seems the most personal, to have least the air of make-believe. An older South and the South of Faulkner's young manhood are in it, the two parts of the history fused and merged into an intensely dramatic vision of the South.

Faulkner's next book, *The Unvanquished*, in some ways a strange volume, is composed of several short stories about the Civil War in Yoknapatawpha County which had appeared in the *Saturday Evening Post*, *Scribner's Magazine*, and elsewhere.[3] But the final story, "Odor of Verbena," was published only in *The Unvanquished*. The volume is composed on the one side of slick magazine stereotypes of the Confederate soldier and the unquestioned romanticizing of the Sartoris males, but on the other it contains a few nightmarish scenes of the anguished days of the South's

* Faulkner's mythical county, Yoknapatawpha, takes its name from a neighboring river and county, Yocana, pronounced Yokny, and in earlier years written Yocanapatapha.

defeat and, at the book's end, a very cold, quizzical view of the old order.[4]

In *Sartoris* there are scenes in which the dashing Bayard, an ancestor who fought with Jeb Stuart, is gallant and courageous and headlong. But there is no attempt to probe the moral center of his actions, or indeed of the old order itself. Although there is this at least curious exchange between Grandfather Bayard Sartoris (who is the boy Bayard in *The Unvanquished*) and a Civil War veteran: "Old Bayard shook the ash from his cigar. 'Well,' he said, 'what the devil were you folks fighting about, anyway?' 'Bayard,' old man Falls answered, 'be damned ef I ever did know.' " Nor does *The Unvanquished*, until the final story, do much probing into the values in the old order. It has little to do, incidentally, with the ante-bellum world — its setting is northern Mississippi toward the War's close and later.

The earlier stories are filled with Tom Sawyerish adventures of a white boy, Bayard, and Ringo, a colored boy, who wage their own war against the Yankees and who watch, mostly at a distance, the exploits of John Sartoris, Bayard's father. They also accompany pious and upright Granny Millard when she undertakes to outwit the Yankees. In "Riposte in Tertio," a slightly more serious story, Granny Millard is killed by a bushwhacking companion of Ab Snopes named Grumby, and the boys, now about fifteen years old, pursue Grumby and Bayard shoots him.

"Skirmish at Sartoris," the sixth story, is nominally about the marriage of John Sartoris and Drusilla, the beautiful Amazon who, dressed like a man, had been fighting in John Sartoris' troop. Propriety, according to local female opinion, requires that Drusilla be married to John, even though it is quite clear that their relationship has been perfectly chaste. The marriage is interrupted to enable John Sartoris to drive away carpetbaggers and prevent Negroes from voting. After allowing, in true gallant fashion, two male Burdens (their story is told by Joanna in *Light in August*) to shoot at him first, Sartoris kills them. Sartoris, of course, disenfranchises the Negro — but this is not considered even briefly. The action is turned sharply back to Aunt Louisa's shocked surprise

101

that anything should have postponed her daughter Drusilla's becoming an honorable woman. Perhaps there is a strong case to be made for disenfranchisement at that point in southern history. If there is, Faulkner passed up an opportunity to dramatize it. Sartoris seems a cardboard "hero," moving inside a stereotyped, thoughtless action.

The final story, "Odor of Verbena," presents Bayard, now a young man of college age, looking at such actions through mature eyes. Drusilla is made to voice the belief that John Sartoris lives the way a man should live and has the welfare of his section at heart: "There are not many dreams in the world, but there are a lot of human lives." The lives, she adds, are worth little – the dream is worth everything. But Bayard, although tempted by the notion, does not believe she is right. He sees his father as too much given to headlong heroics. His pride, his dream of honor, has caused him to kill other men – so that he finally is unable to live easily with himself. He invites his own death from a man (it is the Falkner family story again), Ben Redlaw, whom he has treated contemptuously.

After Redlaw has killed John Sartoris, Bayard sees that he is expected to kill Redlaw in turn. The way Faulkner characterizes the men who expect the new killing is instructive. Bayard says in looking at a group of them that they gathered with that "curious vulture-like formality which southern men assume in such situations." They attend Bayard with "that unctuous and voracious formality." He refuses to shoot at Redlaw, even though, to satisfy himself that he is not without courage, he gives Redlaw the opportunity, which is not taken, to shoot at him. And he comes to see that Drusilla, who makes love to him despite being married to his father, is acting out her own romantic voraciousness – a living legend that love belongs with danger and courage. Bayard has a margin of admiration for the dream with which his father had lived, but he knows that it invited arrogance, theatricality, heroics, violence, and even murder.

The Unvanquished begins as a picture-book story of the glorious heroism of a people at war but ends with the recognition that

Consequences of the Old Order

heroics, in the words of Aunt Jenny, are "for small boys or fool young women." The reader wonders whether the concluding story was present to Faulkner's mind throughout the writing of the earlier stories, or whether the need for it was borne in upon him as he studied what he had written. In addition to the Burdens, many Yoknapatawpha figures appear in *The Unvanquished*: Uncle Buck, Thomas Sutpen, General Compson, Ab Snopes, and so on. It is conceivable that the air of unreality they took on in the presence of the Sartoris legend made Faulkner take another, a closer, look at the legend itself.*

* Professor Arthur Palmer Hudson has written: "Through one of the most remarkable ironies of history, this war was apotheosized and enshrined the shadow of the old order for fifty years." [5]

Two Types of Love

B Y AND LARGE the critics of Faulkner's fiction in the 1930s saw his complications in plot and complexities in sentence structure as perverse, his subject matter as bizarre, and his moral insight as of dubious value. His reputation was good abroad, especially in France, but his status in American letters seemed at least unresolved.[1] With the publication of *The Wild Palms*,[2] however, there was a renewal of interest in his work. Southern literature, long in the doldrums, had in recent years produced significant poets, novelists, and critics and in the *Southern Review* had a literary magazine called by T. S. Eliot the best in the United States. If the southern renaissance was a major literary movement, then the literary world had to come to terms with Faulkner, who undoubtedly was its major novelist. Whether for this or other reasons, *Time* ran a picture of Faulkner, in parachute regalia, on the cover of a January 1939 issue and devoted a three-page article to his career and a review of his latest book.[3]

"In Oxford," the article reads, "he lives quietly, writes, rides, hunts or drives his tan Ford to his 35-acre place in the hills. His daughter Jill, five-and-a-half, wakes him about seven, and after reading her the funnies in the Memphis *Commercial Appeal* at breakfast he works until about eleven. . . . Sitting in his study he talks eloquently, intently in sentences that sound old-fashioned

and literary, about hunting horses, Sherwood Anderson, Colonel
Falkner, Don Quixote, flying, the ways of Negroes in winter, cotton, tenant farming, his daughter Jill, the changing South. A landlord, a conservative Democrat, he says he finds it too difficult to
run his own place (he has five tenants) to theorize about tenant
farmers, politics, or economics."

The Wild Palms is composed of two separate stories, "Old Man,"
about the Mississippi in flood, and "The Wild Palms," about a
disastrous love affair. There is no plot connection between the two
stories despite Faulkner's having alternated the chapters of them.
When asked, some years later, what the connections were, Faulkner replied disarmingly that each story was too brief for book
publication separately — so he alternated the chapters!* There is
enough similarity in theme, however, to invite comparisons and
contrasts between the two stories — perhaps the most useful contrast being that the tall convict of "Old Man" defines himself as a
moral creature inside the restraints he is confronted by, whereas
the lovers of "The Wild Palms" strive to escape from all the restraints that they see as threats to the absoluteness of their love.
Faulkner, at the time he explained his alternating the chapters, did
say the stories treat "two types of love." 4

The tall convict, with the blue outraged eyes of Faulkner
protagonists, is one of the most admirable figures Faulkner has
created. With other prisoners from the prison farm at Parchman,
Mississippi, he is called out to help during the flood of 1927, when
for six weeks twenty thousand square miles of Mississippi were
under water, and hundreds of thousands of people were driven
from their homes, many of them suffering enormous losses in
property and animal life. With another convict, he is given a skiff
and ordered to find a woman sitting in a cypress in a bayou and a
man on the roof of a cotton house.

When the boat is caught in a violent swirl the second convict
pulls himself from it into a tree. He believes and reports that his
companion has been drowned and the prison authorities make an

* In their paper-covered editions the two stories are published separately,
and Cowley in *The Portable Faulkner* published "Old Man" separately.

official record of the death. The tall convict finds the woman, eight months pregnant, and attempts to return with her. But they are carried madly back and forth by the water, up to Vicksburg and down below Baton Rouge; the convict is shot at by a drunken boatman who can't understand why a convict doesn't want to escape, and again by soldiers to whom he tries to surrender; he and the woman land on a snake-infested Indian burial mound, where the child is born; in Cajun country the convict helps a non-English-speaking Cajun to hunt alligators; when the levee is to be dynamited, they begin to make their way up the Mississippi, stopping to earn money plowing or working at a lumber mill. Finally, at the point where his adventures had begun, the convict surrenders the woman, saying, "Yonder's your boat, and here's the woman. But I never did find that bastard on the cotton house." For their own political reasons the authorities sentence the tall convict to an additional ten years, and as the action ends he is sitting in a bunkhouse regaling his fellow convicts with the story of his adventures.

The power of the story is partly in the impressionistic language of its telling as well as in the river as a symbol of the ill-understood forces against which men like the tall convict successfully contend. He first sees the river from the top of the levee:

He stood in quiet and amazed surmise and looked at the rigid steel-colored surface not broken into waves but merely slightly undulant. It stretched from the levee on which he stood, further than he could see — a slowly and heavily roiling chocolate-frothy expanse broken only by a thin line a mile away as fragile in appearance as a single hair, which after a moment he recognized. *It's another levee*, he thought quietly. *That's what we look like from there. That's what I am standing on looks like from there.*

The sudden disappearance of the boat and the tall convict into the water is described as "a tableau snatched offstage intact with violent and incredible speed," and a line of telephone poles in a flooded cotton field is "a wading millepede." The violence of the river itself is caught in many images: the skiff tries to climb a curling wall of water like a cat, and a flood of racing water, ten feet higher than it had been a moment before, is "curled forward upon itself like a sheet of dough being rolled out for a pudding." The woman in the skiff becomes for the convict "one single inert monstrous sentient womb which, he now believed, if he could only turn his gaze away and keep it away, would disappear." When he climbs the levee on his return, weeks later, he observes "the tide line of the old raging, dry now and lined, traversed by shallow and empty cracks like foolish and deprecatory senile grins."

The tall convict is a man of great courage and almost unbelievable endurance. As a naïve young man — he is only twenty-six after serving seven years of his sentence — he had read too many paperbound adventure stories and undertaken to hold up a train, but that was a mistake he was paying for. Now he was concerned with "his good name, his responsibility not only toward those who were responsible to him but to himself, his own honor in doing what was asked of him, his pride in being able to do it, no matter what it was." Like Byron Bunch or Lena Grove, Faulkner's simple country people, he is polite, considerate, reserved. The Cajun who makes a living catching alligators readily accepts the tall convict and the woman, despite his inability to communicate with them, "divining through pure rapport of kind for kind, hill-billy and bayou-rat, the two one and identical because of the same grudged dispensation and niggard fate of hard and unceasing travail." They ask for nothing in the way of future ease or security — "but just permission to endure and endure to buy air, to feel sun for each little while."

It is out of such spirit that the tall convict attacks and kills his first alligator with a knife, calling forth the excited admiration of the Cajun. It is out of this spirit that he is able to get the woman to the Indian mound where the child is born, and he looks down at it, thinking: "*And this is all. This is what severed me violently from all I ever knew and did not wish to leave and cast me upon a medium I was born to fear, to fetch up at last in a place I never saw before and where I do not even know where I am.*" His good name and his responsibility prevented his leaving her, just as they prevented his wanting to escape. When the woman, seeing water moccasins in the boat, screams, the convict cries out at her, "Hush! I wish I was a snake so I could get out too."

The tall convict is described thus at the end of the story as he talks with his bunkmates: "The other did not move, jackknifed backward between the two bunks, grave and clean, the cigar burning smoothly and richly in his clean steady hand, the smoke wreathing upward across his face, saturnine, humorless, and calm." One can accept it as the description of a man who could approach a deputy hundreds of miles, infinite effort, and weeks after he had received an order, and say to him: "Yonder's your boat, and here's the woman. But I never did find that bastard on the cotton house."

Faulkner is not saying, of course, that there are many like the tall convict, no more than he had said there are many like Addie Bundren. When the man is first thrashing in the water, after the boat has struck him in the face with the violence of a mule and is spinning like a thistle bloom or a wind vane on the surface, he muses "with impotent fury upon that arbitrariness of human affairs which had abrogated to the one [the other convict] the secure tree and to the other the hysterical and unmanageable boat for the very reason that it knew that he alone of the two of them would make any attempt to return and rescue his companion." Like certain others of Faulkner's characters, he is made of durable stuff — courage, persistence, and self-respect.

The river in "Old Man" is as much a created symbol of violence as Addie Bundren's vision of "blood boiling through the land." It is evoked by the rhetorical language and the experiences on it of the tall convict. As Addie fulfills her obligation to the blood and so can get ready to die, he fulfills his and can enjoy then the firm, hard substance of the earth he plowed, the sun he felt on his flesh, and the air he breathed. The river is a symbol of nature or man's lot, implacable and hard but ultimately resistible.

The theme of the love story, "The Wild Palms," is stated early in the action by Charlotte Rittermeyer: "love and suffering are the same thing and . . . the value of love and suffering is the sum of what you have to pay for it and anytime you get it cheap you have cheated yourself." She and her lover pay dearly for it, she with her life, he with a fifty-year prison sentence. And they pay dearly for it during their lives together.

Charlotte Rittermeyer gives up her two children, a comfortable life, and a pleasant (but unloved) husband for it. Wilbourne, a young intern, gives up his career. Both of them give up any possibility of security, believing that making money and wanting things for themselves and each other threaten to consume their love. Wilbourne says there is no place for love in the world today. "It took us a long time, but man is resourceful and limitless in inventing too, and so we have got rid of love at last just as we have got rid of Christ."

In Utah, where they endure the hardships of a harsh winter, Charlotte becomes pregnant. They move to Texas, Louisiana, and Mississippi in search of work but Wilbourne can get only a ten-dollar-a-week WPA job. Because of their poverty, which she is unwilling to impose on a child, Charlotte insists against Wilbourne's protests that he perform an abortion. Through his nervousness and because they have waited too long, the operation is bungled. In a little Mississippi town on the Gulf Coast — where the story opens and ends — Charlotte dies. The doctor who attends her has lived a loveless life and takes grim pleasure in demanding that Wilbourne be punished. Wilbourne is arrested, tried, and sentenced to fifty years at hard labor. During the trial one hears the citizens in the courtroom mutter angrily against Wilbourne and threaten Francis Rittermeyer, Charlotte's husband, when he asks the court to be lenient with the accused. They are a kind of chorus jeering and mocking such dedication to love. Society is the villain, but the tragic couple also are guilty of a kind of *hubris*, trying to live solely or exclusively for love.

The story can be read as the tragedy of love in the modern world, but it probably should be read primarily as the tragedy of love in the physical world, in nature. As the "Old Man" is the symbol of nature for the tall convict, the wind and the dry clashing of the wild palms are the symbols of an alien nature confronted by lovers. Early in the story the autumn wind on a lake shore in Michigan and, later, winter gales at the mine in Utah seem to threaten the lovers. And it is the palms, not the voices of society, that are the true chorus. When Wilbourne in the opening chapter (characteristically, remarks made in the early pages cannot be fully understood until further information is given, piecemeal, throughout the story) calls on the doctor in the neighboring cottage to examine Charlotte, he is seen standing "in the darkness, in the strong steady seawind filled with the dry clashing of invisible fronds." En route to the little town where Charlotte will die, the lovers are aware of the palms: "the scaling palm trunks fled constantly past." When she dies, Wilbourne imagines the sound of the palms: "He could hear the black wind again, risible, jeering, constant, inattentive, and it even seemed to him that he could hear the wild dry clashing of the palms in it." And in jail, after refusing to take the cyanide tablet brought him by Francis Rittermeyer, Wilbourne thinks of love being overcome, not by the difficulties put in its way by society, but by nature, by the decay of the flesh itself:

But after all, memory could live in the old wheezing entrails: and now it did stand to his hand, incontrovertible and plain, serene, the palm clashing and murmuring dry and wild and faint and in the night he could face it, thinking *Not could. Will. I want to. So it is the old meat after all, no matter how old. Because if memory exists outside of the flesh it won't be memory because it won't know what it remembers so when she became not then half of memory became not and if I become not then all of remembering will cease to be. — Yes,* he thought, *between grief and nothing I will take grief.*

10

Frenchman's Bend and the Folk Tradition

Discussions of Faulkner as a traditionalist, the unhappy commentator on the disintegrating world of the Compsons, de Spains, and Sartorises, sometimes imply that he looks down on the descendants of the nonslaveholding class. In the background as *The Hamlet* opens one sees the gutted shell of what once had been a plantation house, literally hewn from the jungle of cypress, which now has all but taken it back. This might seem to invite a contrast between the planter aristocracy and the "rednecks," like Will Varner, who now owns the Old Frenchman's Place.[1] But the story does not present such poles; it does not set a glorious ante-bellum world against a degenerate modern world which has lost the traditional virtues. Some of the citizens of the modern world, like Ratliff, the sewing machine agent, are decent, self-respecting people. They also possess such virtues as generosity, honesty, and good manners. Ratliff and his kind do not represent culture in the usual sense of that term, but they are a folk society and possess the "culture" appropriate to it.

It is a serious distortion of the fictional world of Faulkner to set up the Past, identifying it with the planter aristocracy, and oppose this to the Present, identified with a modernism of self-interest and the pursuit of sensation. Interestingly enough, Ab Snopes, horse thief, was a part of the Civil War community; he did not spring full-bodied from the forehead of Modernism.

The myth of the planter aristocracy presents a society dedicated to personal honor, courage, gallantry, and graciousness. Professional life for members of this aristocracy was restricted to agriculture, the law, and politics. A few great personalities emerged, most of whom are now a part of the history and legend of the Civil War. In a few localities, particularly in the older states, this culture undoubtedly achieved a high degree of the kind of perfection possible to it. But the part of Mississippi with which Faulkner has concerned himself was composed of frontier communities. When the War began, Oxford had been chartered only twenty-four years.

Thus the golden legend of a society of gallant gentlemen in velvet and gracious ladies in crinoline has almost no place in Faulkner's fiction. In *Go Down Moses* the journal "records" kept by the Edmondses and McCaslins, members of the planter or slaveholding class, suggest a minimum of formal education, and their lives are seen as earthy and full of hard work, a far cry from the graciousness of society in Virginia or the low country of South Carolina. The tenant farmer and small merchant classes are not presented as having anything to gain from the old order, either economically, politically, or socially. Nor are the slaves, except for a few in *The Unvanquished,* presented as cheerful children in the willing service of the white master. When Isaac McCaslin looks into the records of his family, he finds most of the slaves and ex-slaves struggling to live as self-respecting free human beings.

Arthur Palmer Hudson, one of Faulkner's Oxford friends, has written the following about the average southerner's attitude toward the Civil War:

The slave-owning aristocracy was driven by the circumstances of its own position to accept the Civil War, as a last desperate measure to preserve itself and the ancient order. Whatever our state papers and the utterances of our public men of the South may reveal as to the ultimate responsibility for that holocaust, every Southerner who has talked intimately with the plain people who survived the struggle has good reason to believe that those who did not own slaves, those who were offered as cannon fodder, did not want it. A smouldering resentment against the North and Northerners there was; but how much of this feeling was due to dim realization of the intolerable situation in the South, and how much was due to the propaganda of slave-owners will never be known. But that there were few illusions among thoughtful common people as to the real issues of the controversy seems reasonably sure. I have never heard the cynical epithet "rich man's war and poor man's fight" applied to the Civil War in a public speech, nor have I seen it in a popular history; but I have heard it many times from the lips of ex-Confederate soldiers.[2]

Mr. Hudson is pretty hard on the heirs of the old feudal aristocracy, accusing them of disenfranchising most of the state's citizens and propagating a bogus legend (as opposed to the down-to-earth heroism of many southerners during the War) about the ante-bellum society:

What I mean by the legend of the Old South is the superstition that a social system founded upon slavery, stratified into castes, dedicated to privilege, and motivated in its public conduct by the pompous absurdities of neo-chivalry, was a perfect society; that the period before the war was a golden age; and that human character reached its perfection in the Old South by and through the system.

The descendants of the planter class, as noted earlier, controlled the political system in Mississippi until the 1920s, when a change in the primary law made the tenant farmer's vote equal in value to anyone's vote. Faulkner's own family was involved in this movement, the rise of the "redneck." Undoubtedly the shift in political control, despite the frequent exploitation of people unaccustomed to the privilege and obligations of the franchise, helped to bring about profound changes in Mississippi life: crop rotation, dairying, small industries, better schools, and an increased awareness of what was anachronistic, pompous, and insincere in the remnants of the old order.

The opening pages of *The Hamlet* clearly identify the citizens of Frenchman's Bend and Beat Four* as descendants of the non-

* A *beat* is the route or area for which a sheriff is responsible. In both *The Hamlet* and *Intruder in the Dust* the officer is Sheriff Hampton.

slaveholding class. These people — with home-made whisky stills and Protestant psalm books — had come originally from the northeast, through the Tennessee mountains. Most of them had Scottish, English, and Welsh names: Turpin, Haley, Whittington, McCallum, Bookwright, Murray, Leonard, Armstid, and Littlejohn. To quote from *The Hamlet*:

They brought no slaves and no Phyfe and Chippendale highboys; indeed, what they did bring most of them could (and did) carry in their hands. They took up land and built one- and two-room cabins and never painted them, and married one another and produced children and added other rooms one by one to the original cabins and did not paint them either, but that was all. Their descendants still planted cotton in the bottom land and corn along the edge of the hills and in the secret coves in the hills made whiskey of the corn and sold what they did not drink. Federal officers went into the country and vanished. Some garment which the missing man had worn might be seen — a felt hat, a broadcloth coat, a pair of city shoes or even his pistol — on a child or an old man or woman. County officers did not bother them at all save in the heel of election years. They supported their own churches and schools, they married and committed infrequent adulteries and more frequent homicides among themselves and were their own courts, judges and executioners. They were Protestants and Democrats and prolific; there was not one negro landowner in the entire section. Strange negroes would absolutely refuse to pass through it after dark.

Most of the figures in *The Hamlet* are viewed sympathetically. Ratliff, whose humorous folk idiom carries a large part of the story, is shrewd, well disposed, and a strong moral voice. Bookwright is a man of character. Most of the women, like Mrs. Armstid and Mrs. Littlejohn, are patient and kindly. And the Tulls are treated with respect. The Varners — Will, the father, Mrs. Varner, Jody, and Eula — are vulgar, earthy, and not especially honest, but their weaknesses bear at least a vague relationship to the norms of human feeling. In comparison with Flem Snopes, they seem, as they would not in most comparisons, almost decent.

The Hamlet centers on Flem, son of Ab Snopes, the horse thief in *The Unvanquished.*[3] Ab's career echoes through *The Hamlet*, especially in Ratliff's recollections of his own childhood experiences. Ratliff also recapitulates parts of the short story "Barn Burning,"[4] which presents the terrible anguish of Sarty (Colonel Sartoris) Snopes, Ab's son and Flem's younger brother, when he repudiates his father and runs away. The boy is treated with profound sympathy. Wisely Faulkner did not incorporate the entire story in *The Hamlet*. The reader's sympathy for the boy would be foreign to the cold contempt or at least uneasiness which is aroused by the Snopeses who people *The Hamlet*. Ratliff focusses attention on the despicable Ab and Flem, almost completely ignoring the boy, merely observing that he has disappeared.

At the opening of *The Hamlet*, Ab's family, his wife, sister-in-law, two daughters, and Flem, are seen becoming the tenants of one of the Varner farms. Ratliff, appearing soon thereafter, informs Jody that Ab Snopes is a barn-burner. Jody, who is used to intimidating his tenants, finds himself intimidated. Wanting to ingratiate himself, Jody rides out to see the Snopes family. This is a part of his exchange with Ab Snopes:

"Evening," Varner said, realising too late that he was almost shouting. "Evening, ladies." The man turned, deliberately, holding a hammer — a rusted head from which both claws had been broken, fitted onto an untrimmed stick of stove wood — and once more Varner looked down into the cold impenetrable agate eyes beneath the writhen overhang of brows.

"Howdy," Snopes said.

"Just thought I'd ride up and see what your plans were," Varner said, too loud still, he could not seem to help it. I got too much to think about to have time to watch it, he thought, beginning at once to think, Hell fire. Hell fire, again, as though proving to himself what even a second's laxity of attention might bring him to.

"I figure I'll stay," the other said. "The house aint fitten for hogs. But I reckon I can make out with it."

"But look here!" Varner said. Now he was shouting; he didn't care. Then he stopped shouting. He stopped shouting because he stopped speaking because there was nothing else to say, though it was going through his mind fast enough: Hell fire. Hell fire. Hell fire. I dont dare say Leave here, and I aint got anywhere to say Go there. I dont even dare to have him arrested for barn-burning for fear he'll set my barn a-fire.

A few minutes later Jody meets Flem:

"Howdy," he said. "You're Flem, aint you? I'm Varner."
"That so?" The other said. He spat. He had a broad flat face. His eyes were the color of stagnant water. He was soft in appearance like Varner himself, though a head shorter, in a soiled white shirt and cheap gray trousers.
"I was hoping to see you," Varner said. "I hear your father has had a little trouble once or twice with landlords. Trouble that might have been serious." The other chewed. "Maybe they never treated him right; I dont know about that and I dont care. What I'm talking about is a mistake, any mistake, can be straightened out so that a man can still stay friends with the fellow he aint satisfied with. Dont you agree to that?" The other chewed steadily. His face was as blank as a pan of uncooked dough. "So he wont have to feel that the only thing that can prove his rights is something that will make him have to pick up and leave the country next day," Varner said. "So that there wont come a time some day when he will look around and find out he has run out of new country to move to." Varner ceased. He waited so long this time that the other finally spoke, though Varner was never certain whether this was the reason or not:
"There's a right smart of country."

Ratliff, however, explains to the Frenchman's Bend folks that Ab Snopes as a younger man — when Ratliff was eight years old and Ab's neighbor — had not been so despicable as he is now. For his audience, sitting on the veranda of Littlejohn's weatherbeaten two-story "hotel," Ratliff explains what it was that had soured Ab.

He tells a long anecdote about Ab's inability to prevent his being taken advantage of by shrewd horse traders. The story is reminiscent of one greatly admired by Poe, A. B. Longstreet's "The Horse Swap," in *Georgia Scenes* (1835).[5] Longstreet has a shrewd dealer in horse flesh, Blossom, revel in having swapped a horse which has, hidden under its blanket, a large incurable sore but which to onlookers and to its new owner, Peter, seems wonderfully agile and responsive. To suggest his good will Blossom adds three dollars to his part of the bargain. Once the swap is made the sore is discovered, and Blossom brags to the new owner that he must be acknowledged "a leetle of the best man at a horse-swap that ever catched a coon." Then it is revealed that the horse Blossom has received in exchange is both blind and deaf. The would-be fleecer is fleeced.

Faulkner's anecdote is much more complicated — there are several people involved in several swaps — and as a tall tale it is more genuinely hyperbolic. The most significant situation is Ab's being traded back his own horse, so painted and swollen that he doesn't recognize it. Ratliff recalls his driving it home in the rain, with Ab, who has drunk a great deal of corn liquor that day, asleep in the wagon, indifferent to the rain pelting his face:

"So I just drove under the first roof I come to and shaken Ab awake. The rain had cooled him off by then and he waked up sober. And he got a heap soberer fast. 'What?' he says. 'What is it?'

"'The horse!' I hollered. 'He's changing color!'

"He was sober then. We was both outen the wagon then and Ab's eyes popping and a bay horse standing in the traces where he had went to sleep looking at a black one. He put his hand out like he couldn't believe it was even a horse and touched it at a spot where the reins must every now and then just barely touched it and just about where his weight had come down on it when he was trying to ride it at Stamper's, and next I knowed that horse was plunging and swurging. I dodged just as it slammed into the wall behind me; I could even feel the wind in my hair. Then there was a sound like a nail jabbed into a big bicycle tire. It went *whishhhhhhhhh* and then the rest of that shiny fat black horse we had got from Pat Stamper vanished. I dont mean me and Ab was standing there with just the mule left. We had a horse too. Only it was the same horse we had left home with that morning and that we had swapped Beasley Kemp the sorghum mill and the straight stock for two weeks ago."

A bicycle pump had been put under the horse's foreshoulder, swelling it to proportions that made it unrecognizable. The anecdote tells us little enough about Ab Snopes before he was "curdled," but it suggests a good deal about Ratliff's manner, and about the characteristic humor of the tenant farmers, livestock traders, and drummers among whom he lives.

Flem, of course, is the chief agent in his clan's rise to power in the Varner store and tenant farm system and in Frenchman's Bend generally. But there is also sententious, weasel-like I. O. Snopes, who takes over the blacksmith shop and later becomes the schoolteacher for the community, leaving the shop for his stupid, good-natured, but conniving cousin Eck, the father of Wall Street Panic Eck. There is ruthless Mink Snopes, a tenant farmer who kills his neighbor, Houston, and there is his and Flem's cousin, Isaac Snopes, the idiot who falls in love with the cow. The following description of Saint Elmo, the son of I. O. Snopes, suggests the animal-like qualities common to the clan:

The boy crossed the gallery and descended the steps, the tight overalls undulant and reluctant across his flabby thighs. Before he reached the ground, his hand rose from his pocket to his mouth; again his ears moved faintly to the motion of chewing.

"He's worse than a rat, aint he?" the clerk said.

"Rat, hell," Varner said, breathing harshly. "He's worse than a goat. First thing I know, he'll graze on back and work through that lace leather and them hame-strings and lap-links and ring-bolts and eat me and you and him all three clean out the back door. And then be damned if I wouldn't be afraid to turn my back for fear he would cross the road and start in on the gin and the blacksmith shop. Now you mind what I say. If I catch him hanging around here one more time, I'm going to set a bear-trap for him."

The Snopeses are invincible liars and thieves because they recognize almost none of the rules of decency or fair play. They cheat each other, the Varners, the whole community, even the shrewd Ratliff. And they do it so impersonally, so imperturbably that their victims are left stupefied or in helpless and abject rage. There seems to be no way of stopping them until, like rodents, they have destroyed or eaten up everything in sight.

Commenting on Mink Snopes, Ratliff says he seems "to be a different kind of Snopes like a cotton-mouth is a different kind of snake." Flem appears to live free or apart from feelings, his face and voice never indicating an emotion. He is dehumanized, the principle of exploitation personified.

It is true that the Snopes world is contrasted with the non-Snopes world, but the differences inside the Snopes world are im-

118

portant. Ab is embittered — and acts out of a perverse pride. There is something almost admirable in the intensity of his hatefulness, his refusal to acknowledge a gesture of kindness, like Ratliff's giving him a bottle of corn liquor. Mink, who hates Flem, is also embittered.

Eula Varner is the ungirdled goddess of Frenchman's Bend; as though out of Homer or Thucydides, she is seen as "a moist blast of spring's liquorish corruption, a pagan triumphal prostration before the supreme primal uterus"; as fruition's center, "swarmed over and importuned yet serene and intact and apparently even oblivious, tranquilly abrogating the whole long sum of human thinking and suffering which is called knowledge, education, wisdom, at once supremely unchaste and inviolable: the queen, the matrix." She is fertility, the pagan ripening of spring and summer.

Contemptuous of her schoolteacher, Labove, and the other young men who watch her in abject fascination, Eula gives herself to Hoake McCarron, a rakish, swashbuckling young man from another county. When McCarron disappears and the other young men cease to visit her, her family recognizes that she is "in trouble." Jody, long frustrated in his attempt to prevent her mesmerizing young men, wants to shoot her seducer, but Will Varner, who is having an affair of his own with the wife of a tenant, is undisturbed, and his wife, hearing Jody loudly announce Eula's condition, threatens to beat Eula and Jody for disturbing her nap! But there is a social situation involved in Eula's pregnancy — and, as one anticipates, it is Flem Snopes who exploits it. He marries her. The whole community learns the details of the arrangements Flem has made with the Varners: funds to take the newlyweds to Texas, a deed to the Old Frenchman's Place, and even the Varners' buying the wedding license.

Ratliff imagines an encounter between Flem and the Prince of Darkness, the former chewing his dead tobacco and replying in his inflectionless voice to each of the Prince's increasingly frantic questions:

" 'What?' the Prince says. 'Disputed what?' Except that it dont make any noise, and now the Prince is leaning forward, and now he feels that ere hot floor under his knees and he can feel his self grabbing and hauling at his throat to get the words out like he was digging potatoes outen hard ground. 'Who are you?' he says, choking and gasping and his eyes a-popping up at him [Flem] setting there with that straw suitcase on the Throne among the bright, crown-shaped flames. 'Take Paradise!' the Prince screams. 'Take it! Take it!' And the wind roars up and the dark roars down and the Prince scrabbling across the floor, clawing and scrabbling at that locked door, screaming."

Usually in the tales of traffic with the Devil the money- or pleasure-seeker turns into a jack-o-lantern, is carried off, or disappears in smoke.[6] But sometimes the Devil is victimized by his superior or wily foe. Flem Snopes, as one would expect, not merely dupes the Prince of Darkness, he drives him to groveling on the hot floor of hell.

The only solace Ratliff knows in thinking of the splendid girl marrying "the froglike creature which barely reached her shoulder" is that he would never really possess her. In announcing his presence to her father she had said, "'Mr. Snopes', saying it exactly as she would have said Mr. Dog."

Book three of *The Hamlet*, called "The Long Summer," contains the much discussed love of Isaac or Ike Snopes for the cow owned by Houston, along with accounts of Houston's life and that of his murderer, Mink Snopes — all against the backdrop of and involved with the community of Frenchman's Bend.

It is said that the idiot-cow story was heard in Oxford as a crude, pornographic account of rural sodomy, told by a local politician for the amusement of some of his constituents. In Faulkner's mind the story took on a pathetic, gruesome, perverse, and strangely beautiful quality. Ike loves the cow with a devotion that is far greater than any affection between man and woman in Frenchman's Bend. Pages (far too many probably) are given to their love, described in the high rhetoric of courtly love:

But she is there, solid amid the abstract earth. He walks lightly upon it, returning, treading lightly that frail inextricable canopy of the subterrene slumber — Helen and the bishops, the kings and the graceless seraphim. When he reaches her, she has already begun to lie down — first the forequarters, then the hinder ones, lowering herself in two distinct stages into the spent ebb of evening, nestling back into the nest-form of sleep, the mammalian attar. They lie down together.

The context makes it quite clear that the treatment of Ike's love for the cow is a complicated, not a simple irony. The loves of two other men, Houston and Mink, are contrasted with the idiot's love. Both men are grim, bitter, unrelenting, and hard in their dealings with others. The meaning of Houston's life is given repeatedly in terms of his having been formed by a spirit described as "mystical fanatical protestant," and of his ultimate capitulation to a woman whose desire for him was "not for love or passion but for the married state." His five children turn away from him, desert him. Mink's bitterness is attributed to a childhood lived in a series of ill-made rented cabins and to an attempt to escape it which ends with his need to marry a woman who had known innumerable men:

Yet he not only saw that he must compete for mere notice with men among whom he saw himself not only as a child but as a child of another race and species, but that when he did approach her at last he would have to tear aside not garments alone but the ghostly embraces of thirty or forty men; and this not only once but each time and hence (he foresaw even then his fate) forever: no room, no darkness, no desert even ever large enough to contain the two of them and the constant stallion-ramp of those inexpugnable shades.

Houston and Mink invite their own destruction, Houston his death at Mink's hands and Mink the punishment for the murder. Poor Ike's love is affirmation, like profound respect and love for the fruitful earth herself.

The Snopeses, as one would expect, exploit this situation also. Lump (Lancelot) sells space for the villagers to watch the idiot making love to the cow, until Ratliff stops the performances by suggesting that I. O. Snopes might lose his school job because of them. Book three closes with a pathetic and comic scene — of the idiot sitting in the stall that formerly housed the cow and holding a toy effigy of a cow. Eck, the blacksmith, explains why he spent twenty-five cents for the toy: "Yes, I felt sorry for him. I thought maybe anytime he would happen to start thinking, that ere toy one would give him something to think about."

The two major episodes in "The Peasants," book four, demonstrate fully Flem's mastery over Frenchman's Bend. In the first, the famous story "Spotted Horses," Flem unleashes the fury of untamed and untamable Texas ponies, working only disadvantage to the Texas cowpuncher who has accompanied him to sell the ponies, bringing a broken leg to Henry Armstid, losing Mrs. Armstid's hard-earned five dollars for her and crushing her spirit, knocking Tull unconscious and incapacitating him for a week, as well as destroying his wagon and two mules.

But the Snopeses, lying to protect one another and contemptuously indifferent to the judge who tries to dispense justice, triumph. Theirs is a harsh, even demoniac glee over human stupidity. Parts of the mad action are under the aegis of an eerie moon. No one stands close to Flem, as though — recalling the vision Ratliff had of him defeating the Devil — he is clearly one of the powers of darkness. Outside of human understanding, he is viewed always from a distance. But the scene which best catches the insane violence of a madly unjust world is that in which the pony rushes into the Littlejohn hallway:

A lamp sat on a table just inside the door. In its mellow light they saw the horse fill the long hallway like a pinwheel, gaudy, furious and thunderous. A little further down the hall there was a varnished yellow melodeon. The horse crashed into it; it produced a single note, almost a chord, in bass, resonant and grave, of deep and sober astonishment; the horse with its monstrous and antic shadow whirled again and vanished through another door. It was a bedroom; Ratliff, in his underclothes and one sock and with the other sock in his hand and his back to the door, was leaning out the open window facing the lane, the lot. He looked back over his shoulder. For an instant he and the horse glared at one another. Then he sprang through the window as the horse backed out of the room and into the hall again and whirled and saw Eck and the little boy just entering the front door, Eck still carrying his rope. It whirled again and rushed on down the hall and onto the back porch just as Mrs Littlejohn, carrying an armful of clothes from the line and the washboard, mounted the steps.

It might be that Faulkner found a suggestion for this scene in one of the tall tales known to his region. In George W. Harris' "Sicily Burns's Wedding," from *Sut Lovingood's Yarns* (1867), Sut tells how, to even the score with the Burns family for not inviting him in to dinner, he put a basket over the head of Sock, the Burns' bull, then stood clear while the bull, maddened by bee stings, went lunging through the back door into the house where the Burns family was dining:[*]

. . . Nex he got a far back acrost the room agin the board pertishun; he went thru hit like hit hed been paper, takin wif him 'bout six foot squar ove hit in splinters, an' broken boards, inter the nex room, whar they wer eatin dinner, an rite yere the fitin becum gineral, an' the dancin, squawkin, cussin, an' dodgin begun. . . . Now, the shamshin ove delf, an' the mixin ove vittals begun. They had sot severil tabils together tu make hit long enuf. So he jis' rolled 'em up a-top ove the pile, a-fitin bees like a windmill, wif her calliker cap in one han, fur a wepun, an' a cract frame in tuther, an' a-kickun, an' a-spurrin like she wer ridin a lazy hoss arter the doctor, an' a screamin rape, fire, an' murder, es fas' es she cud name 'em over.

Old Burns mistakenly grabs at the bull, ending up astride it:

. . . A heavy cloud ove dus', like a harycane hed been blowin, hid all the hosses, an' away abuv hit yu cud see tails, an' ainds ove fence-rails a-flyin about; now an' then a par ove bright hine shoes wud flash in the sun like two sparks, an' away ahead wer the baskit a sirklin roun an' about at randum. Brayin, nickerin, the bellerin ove the bull, clatterin ove running hoofs, an' a mons'ous rushin soun, made up the noise. Livly times in that lane jis' then, warn't thar?

In the final chapter of *The Hamlet* Flem Snopes completes his lemming-like conquest of the community. Wanting to sell the Old Frenchman's Place, he renews interest in the old stories of buried

___

[*] The following story in Harris' collection, although not concerned with any subject matter used by Faulkner, does have this as its opening sentence: "I tell you now, I mind my fust big skeer jis' as well as rich boys mind thar fust boots, ur seeing the fust spotted hoss sirkis."[7]

The Tangled Fire of William Faulkner

treasure, thus arousing the cupidity of various prospective buyers. He even buries a few coins in places where they will be discovered. (The legend of buried treasure, incidentally, is mentioned briefly in the opening pages of *Sanctuary*.) The dupes are Armstid, Bookwright, and even Ratliff. Because the latter two have strongly resisted Flem's machinations earlier in the story, their capitulation here gives Flem a total victory. However, they realize they have been duped and are chagrined that they offered so little opposition. Poor Armstid refuses to accept defeat with them, and, as the story ends, he is digging madly, furnishing amusement for curious onlookers. Flem, accompanied by the indifferent Eula and her baby, drives by en route to Jefferson, which has been the scene of other Snopes' victories and occasional defeats. "Snopes turned his head and spat over the wagon wheel. He jerked the reins slightly. 'Come up,' he said."

The Hamlet, though disjointed and in one sense not a novel at all, is one of the great comic books. In part it is indebted to the oral tall tale, but more generally it participates in the ancient tradition of man satirizing his own weaknesses. Flem is personal aggrandizement incarnate, and Ratliff is his shrewd, witty, but fallible opponent. All of Frenchman's Bend are involved in the conflict between the two, for it is also their conflict.

The Wilderness Theme

INEVITABLY, as Faulkner has grown older, the problems of his region have become more and more profoundly intertwined with his own commitments and ideals. To a reporter who interviewed her about Faulkner at the time of the awarding of the Nobel Prize, Mrs. Calvin Brown said, "I think Billy is heartbroken about what he sees, heartbroken about the deterioration of ideals." She felt he has also suffered, as all intelligent southerners do, over their "confusion and mixed-up emotions . . . about the race question."

The book most frequently quoted by critics examining Faulkner's attitudes about modern society and, inevitably, about the race question is *Go Down Moses*.[1] This book of related short stories does mark a profound shift in his work. In place of the sense of doom, of tragic inevitabilities, or of an Old Testament harshness, one finds a sense of hopefulness, a promise of salvation. There are in *Go Down Moses* two loosely related strands of subject matter: the life of the ascetic Isaac McCaslin, the hunter, and the life of Lucas Beauchamp, the son of the mulatto slave who in turn had been the son of Carothers McCaslin, Isaac's grandfather.[2]

The antecedents of Isaac are explained in "Was," the humorous

NOTE: This chapter is reprinted, with modifications, from the original version in *Accent*, vol. 13, no. 1 (Winter 1953), by permission of the editor.

story in which we learn that Uncle Bud and Uncle Buck, Isaac's father, refused to profit from slavery. Isaac himself figures dominantly in "The Old People," "The Bear," and "Delta Autumn." * Two chapters are devoted to Lucas Beauchamp and his family: "The Fire and the Hearth" and "Go Down Moses." Both of these sections, however, relate more directly and intimately to the action in *Intruder in the Dust,* a later novel, than to the chapters devoted to Isaac. The theme implicit in the sections devoted to Lucas Beauchamp is white injustice to the Negro, and the theme implicit in those devoted to Isaac is the nobility of character to be learned from life in the wilderness. In "The Bear" Faulkner attempts to bring the two subject matters and therefore the two themes together, with the wilderness theme dominating.

Immediately preceding "The Bear" is "The Old People," which develops the wilderness theme and introduces us to the significant figure of Sam Fathers, the son of a Negro slave and Ikkemotube or Doom, a Chickasaw chief. Sam and his mother had been sold to Carothers McCaslin, Ike's grandfather.† After the death of Joe Baker, also a Chickasaw, Sam Fathers asks permission to live by himself at the Big Bottom, the hunting grounds on the Tallahatchie River, as a way of recapturing the spirit of the wilderness which flows in his blood. He is joined there during the hunting expeditions by General Compson, Major de Spain, Boon Hogganbeck (who also has Indian blood, but not from a chief), and others.

When Isaac kills his first deer, Sam marks his face with the blood, teaching him to respect and love what he kills. *"I slew you; my bearing must not shame your quitting life."* (As an old man in "Delta Autumn," Ike recalls the story and elaborates its meaning.) On the same day Ike is shown with Sam, waiting to shoot at a deer they know will return to bed for the night. But at another stand

---

* Isaac had appeared as an incidental character in an early story, "A Bear Hunt" (not included in *Go Down Moses*), a comic story which has no thematic relationship to "The Bear."

† Sam Fathers makes an earlier appearance in "A Justice," in *These Thirteen,* in which his paternity is attributed not to Ikkemotube but to a man named Crawford, or Crayfishford. Incidentally, the Sam Fathers of "The Old People" is a stronger character, more aware of his Indian antecedents than of his slave heritage, than the more passive Sam Fathers of "The Bear."

above them they hear a shot, followed by a hunter's horn, and they know Walter Ewell has killed the deer. Sam tells Ike to wait, and this is what they see:

Then it saw them. And still it did not begin to run. It just stopped for an instant, taller than any man, looking at them; then its muscles suppled, gathered. It did not even alter its course, not fleeing, not even running, just moving with that winged and effortless ease with which deer move, passing within twenty feet of them, its head high and the eye not proud and not haughty but just full and wild and unafraid, and Sam standing beside the boy now, his right arm raised at full length, palm-outward, speaking in that tongue which the boy had learned from listening to him and Joe Baker in the blacksmith shop, while up the ridge Walter Ewell's horn was still blowing them in to a dead buck.

"Oleh, Chief," Sam said. "Grandfather."

When Isaac tells his cousin McCaslin Edmonds the story, the latter confirms it, and we infer that the shade of the deer is to be interpreted as the spirit of the wilderness, related not merely to Sam but to all men if they could but rediscover it, and the symbol of an abundant earth eager to produce. "The Old People," then, is a preliminary probing of the subject of the wilderness and man's relationship to it.

The first version of "The Bear," much simpler than the revised version, is the story of the young Ike's initiation as a hunter and his growing awareness of what is to be learned from the wilderness, symbolized by the bear, Old Ben.[3] His two mentors are Sam Fathers and his own father (in the revised version the mentor is his cousin McCaslin Edmonds, sixteen years his senior and the joint heir with Ike of the McCaslin farm). Old Ben is an epitome, an apotheosis of the old wild life known to the Chickasaws before men hacked away at the forests and before they sold a part of these to Jason Lycurgus Compson or anyone else. Nature should be free and abundant. No one has the right to own or sell it. Sam tells Ike that Old Ben won't allow himself to be seen until, without a gun and without giving in to his fear, Ike learns to relinquish himself to the wilderness. This the boy does learn, even to giving up his watch and compass.

127

The Tangled Fire of William Faulkner

Then he saw the bear. It did not emerge, appear; it was just there, immobile, solid, fixed in the hot dappling of the green and windless noon, not as big as he had dreamed it, but as big as he had expected it, bigger, dimensionless, against the dappled obscurity, looking at him where he sat quietly on the log and looked back at it.

Then it moved. It made no sound. It did not hurry. It crossed the glade, walking for an instant into the full glare of the sun; when it reached the other side it stopped again, and looked back at him across one shoulder while his quiet breathing inhaled and exhaled three times.

Then it was gone. It didn't walk into the woods, the undergrowth. It faded, sank back into the wilderness as he had watched a fish, a huge old bass, sink and vanish into the dark depths of its pool without even any movement of its fins.

Several years later, Ike sees the bear again. At the time he has with him a little mongrel, "of the sort called by Negroes a fyce," which tries to attack Old Ben. Ike drops his gun and chases the fyce, picking it up immediately in front of the bear, which without attacking disappears. Then the boy realizes that he has not wanted to shoot the bear. Talking about it with his father, he comes to realize that the bear represents a "wild immortal spirit," related to the endurance, humility, and courage of the hunter in his contest with the wilderness. Old Ben has a fierce pride in his liberty — "Who at times even seemed deliberately to put that freedom and liberty in jeopardy in order to savor them, to remind his old strong bones and flesh to keep supple and quick to defend and preserve them."

In Sam Fathers, Ike has seen in addition to the wild invincible spirit of the bear inherited from his Chickasaw blood the pride and humility of the Negro, the rewards of endurance and suffering. And from the little fyce he has also learned courage. Ike's father (who, incidentally, is not identified as the elderly Uncle Buck of "Was" or of the revised version of "The Bear") sums up the meaning of the boy's meetings with Old Ben: "Courage, and honor, and pride," his father said, "and pity, and love of justice and of liberty. They all touch the heart and what the heart holds becomes the truth." This in general is the meaning of the story: Old

128

The Wilderness Theme

Ben is the wilderness, the mystery of man's nature and origins beneath the forms of civilization, and man's proper relationship with the wilderness teaches him liberty, courage, pride, and humility.

The bear, as Sir James G. Frazer and others have pointed out, has been treated reverently by primitive hunters.* In seeing him walk upright, leave footprints much like a man's, sit up against a tree, and employ a wide range of facial expressions, and yet belong to a nonhuman wilderness, these hunters must have thought the bear a kind of bridge between man as a rational and conscious creature and man as a physical creature dependent on and involved in that same mysterious nature. Obviously the bear almost begs to be treated as a symbol in stories dealing with man's relationship with nature, especially those stories that present the physical world and the creatures in it as sacramental, as manifestations of a holy spirit suffusing all things and asking that man conduct himself in piety and with reverence. The latter view permeates Faulkner's "The Bear."

Such a view is defensible. It recurs throughout literature, having perhaps its most notable expression in English in the poetry of Blake and Coleridge. But it does invite one to sentimentalize nature and it has no very good answer for those who ask how respectful one should be of a bear or any other creature that wantonly would crush one's head or rip off one's limbs. It invites, that is, the puzzled or angry recognition in *Moby Dick* that the beautiful white polar bears can be killers. Some such reservations as these, which must lurk in the mind of even the sympathetic reader, do not destroy Faulkner's story, but they modify one's enjoyment of it. One gives it sympathy but only partial credence.

In general there are two major changes in the revised form of

---

* It seems likely that Faulkner got a hint for his story from T. B. Thorpe's "The Big Bar of Arkansas."⁴ The following passages from Thorpe suggest the similarities between the two stories: (1) "Only one pup came near him, and he was brushed out so totally with the bar's left paw, that he entirely disappeared. . . ." (2) "Yes, the old varmint was within a hundred yards of me, and the way he walked *over that fence* — stranger, he loomed up like a *black mist*, he seemed so large, and he walked right towards me. I raised myself, took deliberate aim, and fired. Instantly the varmint wheeled, gave a

"The Bear." It incorporates an earlier story, "Lion" (not completely successful in its own terms),[5] which tells how Boon Hogganbeck kills the bear when it tries to kill Lion, the courageous dog, and it presents Isaac McCaslin not only in childhood but in his mature years as a noble hunter and as a Christlike figure who repudiates the land because it has been cursed by slavery.

In the revised version of "The Bear" Old Ben takes to wantonly destroying domestic animals, thus making it justifiable that the hunters track him down to kill him. Major de Spain says, "I'm disappointed in him. He has broken the rules. I didn't think he would have done that." In terms of the wilderness theme, two possible reasons for the bear's action suggest themselves: one, the wilderness even in its primeval form is evil as well as good, but there is no justification or preparation for this in the story; second, the wilderness, simply, is taking revenge on man. This latter interpretation is clearly implied by the unsympathetic descriptions of the lumbering interests cutting into the forest. (In "Delta Autumn" there is this: "No wonder the ruined woods I used to know don't cry for retribution! he thought: The people who have destroyed it will accomplish its revenge.") Old Ben strikes back at the agents of civilization and exploitation.

In the first version of "The Bear" the spirit of the wilderness, of course, dominates the action. The story has, as already implied, a kind of *Midsummer Night's Dream* atmosphere: there are difficulties and stupidities but they are under the aegis of Titania and Oberon and at the end no irreconcilable conflicts will remain. Occasionally we hear the voice of hard reality like that of Theseus or of stupidity like that of Bottom, but ultimately the words belong to the realm of moonlight. Because the hunt is not solely a painless

yell, and w*alked through the fence* like a falling tree would through a cobweb." (3) [The bar, like Old Ben, took to taking hogs whenever it wanted to. This causes the hunter to want to destroy the bar. But he has trouble shooting him, as though the animal's life were charmed. Finally he does kill him, too easily, as it seems to the hunter.] "There is something curious about it, I could never understand — and I never was satisfied at his giving in so easy at last. Perhaps, he had heard of my preparations to hunt him the next day, so he just come in, like Capt. Scott's coon, to save his wind to grunt with in dying; but that ain't likely. My private opinion is, that that bar was an *unhuntable bar, and died when his time come.*"

ritual, however, Faulkner has considerable difficulty in incorporating or assimilating the action of "Lion" into the action of "The Bear." Often the hunt demands violence and cruelty. And the hunt, to the extent that animals are not killed out of a need for food, is a violation of the sacramental view of the world implicit in the wilderness theme.

In "Lion" the bear had no symbolic significance. He was simply a creature to be hunted, and there was nothing sacred about him. The theme grew out of the dog as hunter, not the bear as wilderness. "Lion was like the chief of Aztec and Polynesian tribes who were looked upon as being not men but both more and less than men. Because we were not men either while we were in camp: we were hunters and Lion the best hunter of all." [*] In other words, Lion is the ruthless, nonhuman spirit of the kill. At the close of section two of the revised "The Bear" there are these sentences about thirteen-year-old Ike's attitude toward Lion: "So he should have hated and feared Lion. Yet he did not. It seemed to him that there was a fatality in it." The sentences seem to be a plant, suggesting, but without explaining, to the reader that the apotheosis of Lion is not contradicting the apotheosis of Old Ben. But as a matter of fact, it does contradict it. If Ike is the voice of the wisdom to be learned from the wilderness, then indeed he should have been opposed to the spirit represented by Lion.

And now a look at the main action of "Lion." At the center of the story are Lion and Boon Hogganbeck, who is presented pretty much as mindless or childlike and inefficient, possibly to suggest the degeneracy of the old wild spirit of the Indians. Boon is filled with admiration for the untamable Lion. In attacking the bear Lion is mortally wounded. Boon then kills the bear with a knife and, although wounded himself, carries Lion to a doctor who sews him up but cannot save him. The next year Major de Spain declines to hunt in the Big Bottom and the boy Ike, who is in this story also, perceives the reason: Major de Spain cannot bring himself

[*] In "Lion," unlike "The Bear," the story is told from the point of view of a boy who is *not* Ike McCaslin. Ike himself is the boy's mentor, giving him the sort of advice Sam (who does not appear) gives Ike in both versions of "The Bear."

to revisit the ground where Lion, the spirit of bravery and courage, was destroyed. With the death of Lion the spirit of the hunt, the challenge and the chase, had left the woods.

But the conclusion of "Lion," a brilliantly done scene in itself, does not seem to be the inevitable resolution of the previous actions: Despite Major de Spain's decision, the boy visits the woods at the regular hunting season and sees Boon sitting under a tree, hammering violently at a section of his old worn-out gun. Above Boon in the tree the squirrels are racing madly, frantic from the sounds Boon is making in beating on the stock of his gun. Boon's "walnut face" is "wild and urgent and streaming with sweat," and as the boy goes up to him Boon screams at him in "a hoarse, strangled voice: 'Get out of here! Don't touch them! Don't touch a one of them! They're mine!'" Presumably we are to infer that not merely the spirit of nobility but also the spirit of comradeship and mutual help among the hunters has disappeared with the death of Lion, and that Boon's insistence is civilization's almost hysterical insistence on "mine!" But if so, Lion himself, who is ruthless courage, not generosity, is hardly a good symbol of comradeship and cooperation. Old Ben, in his role as majestic overseer of the wilderness, is a more appropriate symbol of these virtues, and Boon's crazy violence, repeated in the revised "The Bear," seems better motivated.

In section IV of the revised version, Faulkner makes an even stronger effort than he had made through the symbolic figure of Sam Fathers to unite the two major themes of *Go Down Moses*, the proper relationship to nature which is to be learned from the wilderness and the injustice to the Negro. The section is about as long as all the other sections taken together. For the most part, it is new material but it incorporates from the first version the meaning of Old Ben as symbol, here giving the remarks made by Ike's father to Ike's cousin, McCaslin Edmonds.

But the section is not exclusively devoted to the boy Ike's learning the significance of the wilderness theme; it is primarily about Ike at twenty-one refusing to inherit property stained by the guilt of slavery, and it is about Ike's subsequent life. There are long conversations between the cousins, at the end of which we know of Grandfather McCaslin's mulatto heirs and their sometimes terrible sufferings, of the country after the Civil War, of McCaslin Edmonds' attempts to help the mulatto heirs, of Ike's marriage to a woman who is unhappy because of his refusal to inherit his share of the family property, and of his living as a carpenter, obviously in imitation of Christ.

In spite of this new material, the reader has only scattered glimpses of the adult Isaac McCaslin, and is never wholly certain what he is to make of him. More than likely he will see Isaac, at least in part, as far too passive a protester against injustice. Ike never seems a particularly good representative of the virtues to be learned from the wilderness because he is ineffectual or inactive in contexts where the virtues he has learned in the wilderness, particularly the respect for liberty, might motivate him to some positive action. For example, he allows McCaslin Edmonds to put a monthly payment in his bank account, the profit from the land he repudiates, and he allows his cousin to meet the family's and therefore Isaac's own obligations to Carothers McCaslin's mulatto heirs. Isaac would absolve himself not merely from the guilt but from the obligations contingent upon the guilt.

In "Delta Autumn," the final section or story in *Go Down Moses*, we see Ike, now in his seventies, immediately confronted by an instance of racial injustice. The evil of old Carothers McCaslin is repeated: Roth Edmonds, the grandson of McCaslin Edmonds, has a child by a mulatto granddaughter of James Buchanan, whose parents had been owned by Uncle Buck and Uncle Bud. Earlier in "Delta Autumn" Ike has been explaining that the right attitude toward nature — for instance, not exploiting the land and not killing does — leads to having the right attitude toward man. But that this does not relate to the present world becomes clear when Ike is more than a little horrified to discover that the Negress would like to marry the father of her child. *"Maybe in a thousand or two thousand years in America,* he thought. *But not now! Not now!"* As a gesture or token of his good will and of his hopes for the future Ike gives her for the illegitimate child the hunting horn inherited from General Compson.

Ike's silent exclamation that it will take one thousand or two thousand years before a marriage of white and mulatto can take place makes it quite clear that the theme of the wisdom to be derived from the wilderness, even in its great prophet Ike, is merely juxtaposed against the theme of the injustice to the Negro. His silent exclamation merely acknowledges, it does not materially modify the injustice.

The inconsistencies in Ike as a character are merely a manifestation of the more general inconsistency that inheres in Faulkner's attempt to treat the subject of slavery and injustice to the Negro in relation to the wilderness theme. Civilization is not an idyllic wilderness or even an idyllic pastoralism; and slavery and injustice are in the context of civilization. The wilderness, however much civilization can learn from it, has to give way for fields and towns; and the problems of civilization, involving struggles for status or power or acceptance and the abuse or destruction of many things that are beautiful in their natural or original state, are much more complicated than they are in the mythical wilderness of which Ike dreams.

Faulkner's treatment of the theme of the wilderness in the first version of "The Bear" is moving, almost hallucinatory in its power to convince us of the existence of a world of no sin, no evil, no injustice. It does convince us, at the least, of the need for us to contemplate such an ideal world. But Faulkner is not willing, apparently, to allow the implications of the wilderness theme, its power to purify, to work as a leaven inside the subject of injustice to the Negro. The treatment of the spirit of the wilderness has no real relevance beyond acknowledging a former and continuing wrong. It relates to a world not merely prior to slavery but prior to civilization. It is a kind of neurotic dream, an escape from rather than an attempt to solve the present injustice.

Sectionalism, and the Detective Story

Both in quantity and in quality Faulkner's fiction in the 1940s had a decided falling off. After *Go Down Moses,** published in 1942, which some readers will want to rate as one of his best works, he published only *Intruder in the Dust* and *Knight's Gambit*. He had, it is true, written very extensively in the 1930s, partially exhausting his subject matter and probably his energies. Later he said that thirty-five to forty-five are the best years for writing fiction. "Your fire is not all used up, and you know more."

During the years from 1942 to 1948 Faulkner published nothing, but his critical reputation continued to grow. Conrad Aiken, Warren Beck, Joseph Warren Beach, Robert Penn Warren, and a few other critics had written perceptive studies of his work, so that the swing in Faulkner criticism was away from depreciation toward appreciation and admiration. In 1944 Malcolm Cowley translated and published a series of articles by André Gide in one of which Faulkner was called "the most important American writer, essentially, powerfully and in the full sense of the word, a Protes-

---

* Faulkner did a stint of many months in Hollywood after the publication of *Go Down Moses*, working for Warner Brothers at five hundred dollars a week on *Battle Cry*, *To Have and to Have Not*, and *The Big Sleep*. When asked by a reporter how he was enjoying Hollywood, Faulkner replied: "I don't like the climate, the people, their way of life. Nothing ever happens

The Tangled Fire of William Faulkner

tant." And Faulkner's stories were appearing regularly in anthologies used as college textbooks. When Cowley edited *The Portable Faulkner* in 1946, however, none of Faulkner's seventeen books was in print. (*The Portable* does not provide a good sense of Faulkner as *novelist* and it overemphasizes Faulkner as *historian*, but it does give a sense of his imaginative power, the variety of his characters, the force of his style, and the haunting legend he has created.) Even so, the literary and novel-reading public was now ready for Faulkner, curious about him, and interested in his work.

In April 1947 Faulkner agreed to meet some English classes at the University of Mississippi, primarily to answer questions. Previously he had stayed away from the campus and had seen little of the faculty. A member of the faculty who had written extensively about him had seen him only once in four years. When the Russian writer Ilya Ehrenburg and his party, touring America, phoned for an interview, saying they wished to spend several days with Faulkner, he declined to see them more than briefly; angered, they departed without seeing him at all.

In the fall of 1948 — when Faulkner was fifty-one — the American Academy of Arts and Letters honored him, along with John Steinbeck and Mark Van Doren, with membership among the fifty living great American writers and artists. When *'48 the Magazine of the Year* sent a photographer to get pictures of Yoknapatawpha County and of Faulkner, he declined to be photographed, saying, "I hope to be the only unregimented and unrecorded individual left in the world." He was also quoted in the *New York Times Book Review* as saying the price of fame was considerable: "[Once] I was a free man. Had one pair of pants, one pair of shoes, and an old trench coat with a pocket big enough for a whiskey bottle. Now I get stacks of letters, asking what I eat for breakfast and what about curves and linear discreteness."

Unfortunately, his next book, *Intruder in the Dust*, did not live

and then one morning you wake up and find you are sixty-five." (It may not be amiss to speculate that such a story as *The Big Sleep* by Raymond Chandler helped turn Faulkner toward, or strengthen his interest in, the detective story. He is said to have been amused at the surprise registered by a visitor in Oxford over the number of detective stories on the shelves of his library.)

up to what Faulkner had shown himself capable of creating Similar in subject matter to *Light in August*, it does what the earlier novel never does; it sentimentalizes a region and it argues a sectional thesis. *Light in August* presents a social wrong, at least as it appeared twenty-some years ago, but it does not explicitly offer a solution; in fact it shows that the wrong is imbedded deeply in the righteousness of a people, and is involved with their profoundest convictions. A reader of *Light in August* undoubtedly is as a social being concerned to correct or modify so terrible an injustice, but he could hardly feel that an easily formulated thesis and a few rules of conduct would suffice to correct it. He would not, that is, feel that the novel had oversimplified the issues for him.

But in *Intruder in the Dust* Faulkner has not fully faced the difficulties and complexities of getting the mores of "Jefferson" in mid-century into the story; he suggests, without explaining, a kind of vacuousness, even wanton violence, behind the lynch mob; on the other hand there is a vague feeling that "human decency" should be a town's driving force in race relationships.

In *Intruder in the Dust* there is, for example, a description of the people going to church on Sunday, but the account is external; it does not tell us what the relation of the church is to the possibility of there being a lynching. There is a clever and perceptive passage about the architecture of churches, about slender belfries which say "Peace," utilitarian belfries which say "Repent," and one which says "Burn." But we do not see the churches as a part of the psychology of the people in their relation to Lucas Beauchamp, the old Negro accused of murdering a white man. Even the burial of Vinson Gowrie apparently has no connection with the church. There is talk of human dignity, but there is no discussion of the soul. If Faulkner is saying that the church is no longer an essential part of the white man's feeling toward the Negro, we should know what has happened to the old emotions; more specifically we should know what the driving forces are behind the new emotions. The novel does not take us deeply into the mores of mid-century Jefferson because Faulkner is distracted by the argument he is directing at his Yankee readers.

The Tangled Fire of William Faulkner

In one of his speeches to his nephew Chick, for instance, Uncle Gavin Stevens explains how the southerner always sees himself in relation to the North:

. . . not north but North, outland and circumscribing and not even being a geographical place but an emotional idea, a condition of which he had fed from his mother's milk to be ever and constant on the alert not at all to fear and not actually anymore to hate but just — a little wearily sometimes and sometimes even with tongue in cheek — to defy. . . . [From the North] there looked down upon him and his countless row on row of faces which resembled his face and spoke the same language he spoke and at times even answered to the same names he bore yet between whom and him there was no longer any real kinship and so there would not even be any contact since the very mutual words they used would no longer have the same significance and soon after that even this would be gone because they would be too far asunder even to hear one another: only the massed uncountable faces looking down at him and his in fading amazement and outrage and frustration and most curious of all, gullibility: a volitionless, almost helpless capacity and eagerness to believe anything about the South not even provided it be derogatory but merely bizarre enough and strange enough.

Uncle Gavin then explains to Chick that the South is the only relatively homogeneous region left in the United States, and the consequent importance of maintaining this homogeneity:

Only a few of us know that only from homogeneity comes anything of a people or for a people of durable and lasting value — the literature, the art, the science, the minimum of government and police which is the meaning of freedom and liberty, and perhaps most valuable of all a national character worth anything in a crisis — that crisis we shall face someday when we meet an enemy with as many men as we have and as much material as we have — and who knows? — who can even brag and boast as we brag and boast.

The Negro, too, according to Uncle Gavin, is the homogeneous man. He has simple and lasting values, the love of children, his hearth, a little piece of land, and the will to endure. The Negro and southern white should confederate. Together they could present "a front not only impregnable but not even to be threatened by a mass of people who no longer have anything in common save a

Sectionalism, and the Detective Story

frantic greed for money and a basic fear of a failure of national character which they hide from one another behind a loud lip-service to a flag."

One may desire the elemental and enduring values that Faulkner desires, and one may admire the wit and the bite in his satire on parts of the American character.* Yet one cannot believe, nor does Faulkner, that the South is or can be free from the materialist-mechanical appeals or temptations to which so many Americans eagerly succumb. Uncle Gavin in another speech for young Chick points out that Jefferson, Mississippi, is not immune (he is discoursing this time on noise):

. . . but mostly and above all the motion and the noise, the radios and the automobiles — the jukeboxes in the drugstore and the poolhall and the cafe and the bellowing amplifiers on the outside walls, not only of the sheet-music store but the army-and-navy supply store and both feed stores and (that they might falter) somebody standing on a bench in the courthouse yard making a speech into another one with a muzzle like a siege gun bolted to the top of an automobile, not to mention the ones which would be running in the apartments and the homes where the housewives and the maids made up the beds and swept and prepared to cook dinner so that nowhere inside the town's uttermost corporate rim should man, woman or child citizen or guest or stranger be threatened with one second of silence.

Again, one may agree with Uncle Gavin that many in the North seem "eager to believe anything about the South not even provided it be derogatory but merely bizarre enough and strange enough" or agree that the press oversimplifies the racial problem, without, however, believing that the federal government should leave the problem completely in the hands of the South.† Uncle Gavin says

* For example, Uncle Gavin on the automobile: "The American really loves nothing but his automobile: not his wife his child nor his country nor even his bank account first (in fact he doesn't love that bank account nearly as much as foreigners like to think because he will spend any or all of it for almost anything provided it is valueless enough) but his motorcar. Because the automobile has become our national sex symbol. We cannot really enjoy anything unless we can go up an alley for it."

† Thus Jean Paul Sartre could write a "successful" play with all the necessary stereotypes, without any firsthand knowledge of the South. All he needed was a little imagination and the information gained from articles in some of our liberal weeklies.

139

The Tangled Fire of William Faulkner

the South is defending the privilege of setting the Negro free, that the Negro is "now tyrant over the whole county's white conscience." This is a nice point; the southerner should relieve his conscience, but North or South there are those without the requisite sensitivity of conscience. The threat of having to legislate justice — granting it is preferable that it remain only a threat — should hurry the work of conscience, shame, and the sense of human decency. Those with the sympathies and insight of Gavin Stevens, Chick, Miss Habersham, Sheriff Hampton, and a few others in the story might on their own achieve, and fairly soon, a just and easy relationship with the Negro, but people like Mr. Lilley, the Gowries, and the Beat Four folks need a little prodding, or even coercion, and it seems too expensive a sentiment to insist that coercion come solely from the collective local conscience.

Again, one questions, as one does not with Hightower in *Light in August*, whether the past, the legend of the South, lives in the mind of a fourteen-year-old southern boy in the middle of the twentieth century, whether

For every Southern boy fourteen years old, not once but whenever he wants it, there is the instant when it's still not yet two o'clock on that July afternoon in 1863, the brigades are in position behind the rail fence, the guns are laid and ready in the woods and the furled flags are already loosened to break out and Pickett himself with his long oiled ringlets and his hat in one hand probably and his sword in the other looking up the hill waiting for Longstreet to give the word and it's still all in the balance, it hasn't happened yet, it hasn't even begun yet, it not only hasn't begun yet but there is still time for it not to begin against that position and those circumstances which made more men than Garnett and Kemper and Armstead and Wilcox look grave yet it's going to begin, we all know that, we have come too far with too much at stake and that moment doesn't need even a fourteen-year-old to think *This time. Maybe this time* with all this much to lose and all this much to gain: Pennsylvania, Maryland, the world, the golden dome of Washington itself to crown with desperate and unbelievable victory the desperate gamble.

Hightower's generation could think it, couldn't help thinking it perhaps; Quentin Compson's generation (which is Faulkner's own) could also think it; and even some in the generations that matured before the beginning of World War II could think it. But to those younger than that the Civil War must seem almost as remote as the Revolutionary War.

One believes in the world brought to life in *Light in August*; it carries its own conviction. One believes only in part in the world of *Intruder in the Dust*. In not recognizing how much the South has changed, becoming more and more like the North, *Intruder in the Dust* does not face the racial problem in the terms in which it now presents itself. Too many speeches obtrude from it. Consequently the point of view seems lacking in depth and intensity; the style, lacking its usual informing fury, seems thin and remote from what should have been its vital sources.

Intruder in the Dust has many of the virtues, although in a lesser degree, of Faulkner's earlier work: the wit, the virtuosity in language, the quality of living figures, the luminous scenes. But the reader does not feel that the true center of the novel is in the relationship between Lucas Beauchamp, the dignified and somewhat willful old Negro falsely accused of murdering a Gowrie, and the white citizens of Jefferson. He may feel that the novel is a brief for the defense, not a novel written for a later as well as a present generation.

Intruder in the Dust clearly suggests that Faulkner is closer to most southern opinion on the way to reduce racial tension than to liberal Yankee opinion. But this does not imply that Faulkner is willing to condone one set of legal practices for the white population and another for the Negro. On one occasion he wrote a letter to the *Commercial Appeal* in strong protest against the slight sentence that was given a white man who had killed three Negro children:

It is to be hoped that whatever reasons they [the jury] may have had for saving him, will be enough so that they can sleep at night free of nightmares about the ten or fifteen or so years from now when the murderer will be paroled or pardoned or freed again, and will of course murder another child, who it is to be hoped — and with grief and despair one says it — will this time at least be of his own color.

141

The Tangled Fire of William Faulkner

He wrote another letter to protest a premeditated and brutal murder of a Negro by three white men who subsequently were declared not guilty. The Negroes, Faulkner said in the letter, were being given a heritage of desperation and hatred. And Faulkner spoke to a Civil Rights Congress delegation, declaring his belief in the innocence of Willie McGee. A number of southern papers attacked Faulkner for defending a guilty man and allowing his name to be used by a Communist front group, but Faulkner said the main issue was that, in his opinion, the man was innocent.

The successful detective story, which Faulkner essayed in his next book, *Knight's Gambit*,[2] lives by its own conventions: the very superior detective; his confidant, from whom he withholds significant information until he is ready to reveal the whole pattern of his shrewd deductions; indifference to the number of deaths or the suffering they entail; the presence of many suspects; the reader's being given a teasing but not a revealing number of clues; the details of the crime having to be imagined by the detective or, through his subtle trickery, confessed; and so on. Such conventions, appropriate to the genre, do not serve verisimilitude, psychological truth, or profound probings into a world view. Contrariwise, a style that employs a subtilized diction, the swell and modulation of appropriate tones, the fullest dramatization of theme, is not necessary for the detective story — and when employed it usually fails because it is out of keeping with the occasion. It may seem pretentious or merely beside the point.

"Smoke," * the opening story in *Knight's Gambit*, is typical of several of the other stories in the collection in that the deduction, upon which the story turns, is tricky and insignificant, whereas most of the characters live grimly, frequently caught by forces urgently compulsive, beyond any easy rational control. "Smoke" is concerned with a violent man, Anselm Holland, who so injures and enrages his son, Anse, that the son leads the life of an eccentric

---

* Surprisingly, the story "Smoke" appeared first in *Dr. Martino*, suggesting that Faulkner's interest in the detective story goes back at least to the very early 1930s.

and hermit after a stormy leave-taking and breaking of all ties with his father; with a second son, Virginius, whose reasonableness and sweetness of temper are of no avail against the father, who demands that he too leave the family home; with one Granby Dodge, a former preacher, cousin of the Holland boys, with whom the second son lives after leaving home; and with other more or less incidental characters. There are two murders: Anselm Holland is found dead and Judge Dukinfield is killed when he appears to have inferred who Holland's murderer was.

All of this and much more comes out as Gavin Stevens addresses a jury. The crime is solved by a not very convincing trick which causes Dodge to confess. The characters and their actions, even though only mediocre Faulkner, are wasted because they are irrelevant to Stevens' sleuthing. There is no thematic significance to the story.

Even more pointless is "Monk," the story of a moron who arouses the sympathies of Gavin Stevens. In the early sections of the story Monk's pathetic history is told: his shiftless and probably criminal parents, his running away after the death of his grandmother, his living with an old man who illegally made and sold whisky, his becoming known to the town —

He was known about town now, in the cheap, bright town clothes for which he had discarded his overalls — the colored shirts which faded with the first washing, the banded straw hats which dissolved at the first shower, the striped shoes which came to pieces on his very feet — pleasant, impervious to affront, talkative when anyone would listen, with that shrewd, foolish face, that face at once cunning and dreamy, pasty even beneath the sunburn, with that curious quality of imperfect connection between sense and ratiocination.

When Stevens learns Monk is innocent of the murder for which he has been sentenced to prison (the actual murderer confesses), he obtains a pardon for him, but Monk likes the warden and refuses to leave the prison. Suddenly, and under circumstances not understandable to Stevens, Monk kills the warden. This sets off the sleuthing expedition, and Stevens solves the case after investigating a strange coincidence, by showing that another prisoner has been shrewd enough to use "the poor bat brain" as his tool.

The pathos of Monk's life, slightly developed though it is, is cheapened by being made merely the occasion for Lawyer Stevens' sleuthing. That Faulkner was not much at ease with the story and strove to give it a significance it does not possess seems suggested by the pretentiousness of the opening paragraph, spoken by Charles Mallison, the young nephew of Stevens:

I will have to try to tell about Monk. I mean, actually try — a deliberate attempt to bridge the inconsistencies in his brief and sordid and unoriginal history, to make something out of it, not only with the nebulous tools of supposition and inference and invention, but to employ these nebulous tools upon the nebulous and inexplicable materials which he left behind him. Because it is only in literature that the paradoxical and even mutually negativing anecdotes in the history of a human heart can be juxtaposed and annealed by art into verisimilitude and credibility.

"Hand upon the Waters" is about the murder of a Lonnie Grinnup and, in turn, the killing of his murderer. This time, too, Lawyer Stevens, thanks to his keen powers of observation, solves the crimes. Lonnie Grinnup is identified as the last of the Greniers — Grinnup is a corruption of that name — who were among the first to settle in Yoknapatawpha County, but this information is not significantly employed.

"Tomorrow" finds Uncle Gavin Stevens trying to find out why Jackson Fentry, an inoffensive, honest, hard-working man, was willing to hang a jury. His reason, Stevens discovers, was that the murdered man, although a brute, bully, and intended bigamist, had as a tiny child been protected and cared for by Fentry. Although the story rests on a rather slight conception and insight, its tone is not seriously disturbed by conventions borrowed from the detective story.

"An Error in Chemistry," on the other hand, depends on a convention. The murderer this time is a former carnival entertainer who is adept at impersonation and at make-up. His vanity impels him to try to impersonate the man he has recently murdered. He makes a mistake, however, which a native would not make: in preparing a glass of whisky he neglects to mix the sugar first in a little water; instead he drops the sugar into the raw whisky where it swirls like sand toward the bottom. This of course causes his apprehension.

The title story, "Knight's Gambit," is a long, tedious account of Gavin Stevens' love for a middle-aged woman. Years earlier he had had the misfortune to enclose in an envelope addressed to her a letter intended for his mistress. When the action opens, she, her lover (she has already been twice married), and her two children are in Jefferson. Stevens, with his inimitable shrewdness, prevents the murder of the lover, a Captain Gualdres, a South American horseman, and helps the daughter to marry Gualdres. He himself, twenty years late, is then free to marry his sweetheart.

Faulkner several times, in this last story, mentions Stevens' garrulousness, but he seems not to recognize that the pontificating on any and all subjects — human foibles, education, literature, politics — destroys the unity of the story. And too often Stevens' voice seems merely a character's remove from Faulkner's own, although occasionally the wonderful rhetoric of Faulkner's earlier style reappears, as in this passage:

. . . the car howling and wailing up the street toward the Square with all the lights burning, parking driving and fog, then blatting and crashing between the brick walls and the street narrowed into the Square; and afterwards he remembered a cat leaping in silhouette across the rushing lights, looking ten feet long one second then the next one high and narrow as a fleeting fence post.

Certainly the genre of the detective story is ill adapted not merely to Faulkner's characteristic language, but to his themes and subject matter.

13

The Right to Responsibility

THE NOVEMBER 16, 1950, issue of the
Oxford Eagle proudly announced that a native son, William
Faulkner, had been granted the 1949 Nobel Prize for literature,
with a cash award of about $30,000. Only three other Americans —
Eugene O'Neill, Sinclair Lewis, and Pearl Buck — had been recipients of the prize.

Some of the newspapers in Mississippi, believing Faulkner had
not served his local region at all well, took exception to his being
given the prize. Major Frederick Sullens, editor of the *North Mississippi Herald*, wrote that Faulkner belonged to the "privy school
of literature," a sentiment echoed in a number of small-town newspapers.

Faulkner himself, after the newspapers announced the prize,
went off on a hunting trip in the Delta Bottoms, on the sort of
expedition described in *Go Down Moses*. Ike Roberts, the chief of
the camp, reported to the press that Faulkner was a good hunting
companion, patient and willing to take his turn in picking up the
"smutty end of a log."

The account in the *Eagle* had quoted Faulkner as saying that
he had not yet decided whether he would attend the ceremonies
in Stockholm. Reported the *Eagle*, "His dislike of attending 'functions' is well known in Oxford. But he is seldom, if ever, rude to

The Right to Responsibility

anyone." Faulkner, of course, did attend the ceremonies, making a speech which was widely acclaimed:

I feel that this award was not made to me as a man but to my work — a life's work in the agony and sweat of the human spirit, not for glory and least of all for profit, but to create out of the materials of the human spirit something which did not exist before. So this award is only mine in trust. It will not be difficult to find a dedication for the money part of it commensurate with the purpose and significance of its origin. But I would like to do the same with the acclaim too, by using this moment as a pinnacle from which I might be listened to by the young men and women already dedicated to the same anguish and travail, among whom is already that one who will some day stand here where I am standing.

Our tragedy today is a general and universal physical fear so long sustained by now that we can even bear it. There are no longer problems of the spirit. There is only the question: When will I be blown up? Because of this, the young man or woman writing today has forgotten the problems of the human heart in conflict with itself which alone can make good writing because only that is worth writing about, worth the agony and the sweat.

He must learn them again. He must teach himself that the basest of all things is to be afraid; and, teaching himself that, forget it forever, leaving no room in his workshop for anything but the old verities and truths of the heart, the old universal truths lacking which any story is ephemeral and doomed — love and honor and pity and pride and compassion and sacrifice. Until he does so, he labors under a curse. He writes not of love but of lust, of defeats in which nobody loses anything of value, of victories without hope and, worst of all, without pity or compassion. His griefs grieve on no universal bones, leaving no scars. He writes not of the heart but of the glands.

Until he relearns these things, he will write as though he stood alone and watched the end of man. I decline to accept the end of man. It is easy enough to say that man is immortal simply because he will endure; that when the last ding-dong of doom has clanged and faded from the last worthless rock hanging tideless in the last red and dying evening, that even then there will still be one more sound: that of his puny inexhaustible voice, still talking. I refuse to accept this. I believe that man will not merely endure: he will prevail. He is immortal, not because he alone among creatures has an inexhaustible voice but because he has a soul, a spirit capable of compassion and sacrifice and endurance. The poet's, the writer's duty is to write about these things. It is his privilege to help man endure by lifting his heart, by reminding him of the courage and honor and hope and pride and compassion and pity and sacrifice which have been the glory of his past. The poet's voice need not merely be the record of man, it can be one of the props, the pillars to help him endure and prevail.

En route to Stockholm by plane, Faulkner had been asked by a reporter in New York what he, known as a specialist in decadence, considered the most decadent thing in America. He replied: "What you're doing, Miss."

The awarding of the Nobel Prize seems to have marked the end of Oxford's antipathy to Faulkner. The town's pride in their native son was expressed by the *Oxford Eagle* in the issue for Thursday, January 4, 1951. A banner headline read, "Welcome Home, Bill Faulkner." Under it were pictures of Faulkner talking with Swedish officials, chatting with a little Swedish child, walking in the snow with his daughter Jill, and so on. Beneath the pictures was this statement: "Just For the Record and to Tell People Everywhere — Oxford, And All of Us, Are Very Proud of William Faulkner, One of Us, The Nobel Prize Winning Author." The statement was signed by thirty-two merchants.

In the same issue of the *Eagle,* there was a review of such 1950 headlines as this: "Nobel Award for Literature of 1949 given to William Faulkner. Grand climax in 30-year career of Oxford's world-famed citizen as Swedish foundation picks him as one of the great writers of all times." And this: "Faulkner hailed as epic writer at Nobel Award ceremony; home folks swell with pride."

In the preceding issue, December 28, daughter Jill had begun a series of feature articles about the trip to Sweden with her father.[1] The articles were devoted to *her* trip, how it all looked to a teen-ager from Oxford, Mississippi. The articles suggested a knowing young lady, capable at once of being awed by the grandeur and the pomp but also amused by overserious officials. "Pappy," as she called him, did not dominate the articles —she treated him affectionately as a small but significant part of the pageant. Thus of the presentation ceremony:

The Hall was beautiful with statutes and tapestries. . . . I was seated in front of the hall with the families of the other award winners; the royal family was seated just in front of us, and then Pappy and the winners were on the platform with their sponsors and the other members of the Academy.

And of a later scene:

At last Pappy and I were ushered into the Throne Room where we talked a few minutes to the King and Queen and to the other members of the royal family and then passed on into a long hall on the other side of the Throne Room where more black liveried footmen served champagne and little cakes.

A few minutes after the last person had been presented, the doors from the Throne Room were thrown open and the Captain of the King's guard or the Lord High Chamberlin or some such important person marched out followed by Their Majesties. A hush fell and everyone bowed low as they moved slowly down the hall, pausing to speak to someone occasionally. The King came and talked to Pappy for a long time about farming, archeology (he is a noted archeologist), sailing, Mississippi, and Sweden and then passed on to speak to the Danish ambassador who was carrying my coat all this time.

Prior to the award Oxonians had looked upon Faulkner as the black sheep of an old family. Even now, if a visitor presses some of them for their opinions of his books he is likely to hear the term "genius," used not to characterize Faulkner's employment of a medium so much as to excuse his frequent offenses against the mores of Mississippi.

However, in the last few years Faulkner has had an easier relationship with his neighbors. He has admitted that his representation of the area has resulted in a misunderstanding of what it actually is. In his more recent books he has shown Oxford and its environs in a much softer light. And in letters to the *Oxford Eagle* he has teased the citizens of such a hard-drinking community for voting dry on the local liquor option. He even printed a broadside answering an advertisement paid for by three Oxford ministers concerned with outlawing the sale of beer in Lafayette County. The broadside began:

1. "Beer was voted out in 1944 because of its obnoxiousness." Beer was voted out in 1944 because too many voters who drank beer or didn't object to other people drinking it were absent in Europe and Asia defending Oxford, where voters who preferred home to war could vote on beer in 1944.

2. "A bottle of four-per-cent beer contains twice as much alcohol as a jigger of whiskey." A twelve-ounce bottle of four-per-cent beer contains forty-eight one-hundredths of one ounce of alcohol. A jigger holds one and one half ounces (see dictionary). Whiskey ranges from thirty to forty-five per cent alcohol.

The remainder of the broadside maintained this same ironical tone and precision of statement. Incidentally, the county maintained the prohibition against the sale of beer.

Occasionally during the earlier years one might have heard the statement, probably only half-seriously expressed, that Phil Stone had written the stories published under the name of William Faulkner. The town knew Faulkner as a man with relatively little formal schooling, and they probably knew that he had been an indifferent student. Stone, a graduate of Yale, had the sort of education the town could accept as requisite for a learned author. It is not too fanciful, however, to conjecture that attributing the fiction to Stone was a way, however ambiguous, of simultaneously exorcising the troublesome young man from its consciousness and of giving him his comeuppance. But that sort of thing, so far as Oxford is concerned, seems to be all in the past. Talking with members of the "better families" now, one is likely to hear comments like the following:

Yes, *Intruder in the Dust* was filmed here in Oxford in 1949. The people from Hollywood were extremely nice. The director and those playing the more important parts were invited to some of the better homes. They were charming, not what one would expect from the stories one hears about Hollywood. Having local folks play in the movie was amusing, but the merchants on the

The Right to Responsibility

square had to ask the company not to pay the extras more than they were getting in the stores — otherwise there would have been no clerks at all. Was the movie true of Lafayette County? No, that colored man, Juan Hernandez, was a Puerto Rican, not like our colored people. Ours are not that intelligent. That final scene, in which Lucas Beauchamp insists upon paying Lawyer Gavin Stevens his fee and on getting his change? No, it is not at all typical of our colored people. Now that there is more money in the South we can do more for them. One must remember that economic recovery after the War was slow. We are trying to do more for them — but that does not mean there can be an end to segregation. . . .

Having the premiere at the Lyric — that's just off the square, over near the high school — was entertaining. Did you know that William wasn't going to attend, at least not until he learned his aunt from Memphis wanted to come down for it? He and his whole family did come. He wore a dress suit, tails 'n' all. The New York papers, by the way, make too much of his being a farmer, wearing only old clothes, not ever having had on formal clothes, and so on. That's to forget what the Falkner family has been. William's father, Murray Falkner, was business manager at the university. William practically grew up on the campus. As a student he was a member of Sigma Alpha Epsilon, a very good fraternity. . . .

William has made a good deal of money in recent years — with the movie, the Nobel Prize, and the increased sale of his books. He has a fine sailboat over on the reservoir, Great Sardis Lake. Sardis is a little town about twenty miles from here. The newspapers shouldn't make so much of his being just a dirt farmer who finds time to write books. . . .

Was he quite poor some years back? He may have been poor, at times, though not terribly poor. He has had his farm for at least twenty years — a good-sized farm. He used to work in the mornings at his writing and oversee the farm in the afternoon. If he was poor, it was the drinking. A man who drinks a great deal — but that is a long time ago now. . . .

151

The Tangled Fire of William Faulkner

Faulkner's close friends, who have known him for many years, insist that stories about his being a Paul Bunyan of the bottle are greatly exaggerated. Letters about him from these friends are likely to read like recommendations addressed To Whom It May Concern: William Faulkner is not only an artist but a gentleman. His attitude toward his friends and neighbors is exemplary. I know of no scandal of any sort about him. . . .

It is clear enough that Faulkner has been an exceedingly patient and hard-working writer. In bulk his fiction is as large as that of any comparable contemporary. The more than nine hundred pages in *Collected Stories*,[2] for example, published in the fall of 1950, make it evident that Faulkner has looked carefully and with brilliant intensity into a variety of worlds: the strange Indian tales from Mississippi's early history; the dirt farmers and mountaineers from the Civil War to the WPA and Pearl Harbor; the "lost generation" and wastelanders; the Sartoris and Compson families; the Negroes; barnstormers and their families; middle-class scenes in Los Angeles, New Orleans, or New York. The shifts in idiom make it quite clear that Faulkner is among the masters: one really "hears" an eight-year-old country boy, the taciturn, humorless mountaineer, the genteel tone of a town lady, a bewildered, tired old slave, or a politician from the state legislature. Faulkner's characters also exist in relation to generations and a community, with children, adolescents, lovers, parents, the aged, cousins, aunts, and neighbors. Most writers give life to a specialized character or set of characters, the remaining figures living only marginally. Faulkner's world is like a Shakespearean play: rich in characters who exist vividly not only in relation to a central set of characters but also in their own terms. Faulkner's towns, cities, and landscapes live, as sound, odor, texture, movement.

Most of the stories in *Collected Stories* are from *These Thirteen* and *Dr. Martino*, but there are a half-dozen newly reprinted. Several of these, under the heading "The Country," make very clear what the values are that Faulkner would have us live by: self-discipline, self-respect, fulfilling obligations that have no cash nexus. A generation that has grown up in an increasingly collec-

The Right to Responsibility

tivized society may feel there is a "reactionary" streak in Faulkner's politics — and there is. But once inside the world of the characters he admires one can appreciate and applaud the virtues he wants reaffirmed. Interestingly, a rather recent speech delivered by Faulkner to his fellow Mississippians contains a passage that might serve as an epigraph for these stories:

I believe that the true heirs of the old tough durable fathers are still capable of responsibility and self-respect, if only they can remember them again. What we need is not fewer people, but more room between them, where those who would stand on their own feet could, and those who won't, might have to.

Faulkner believes in man's "inalienable right to be responsible."

Faulkner's next book, *Notes on a Horsethief*,[3] published by the Levee Press of Hodding Carter and Ben Wasson, continues one of the themes from "The Country" group of short stories.

In *Notes on a Horsethief* Faulkner has a passage about the hope for man represented by the vast continent of America which is reminiscent of a passage in *The Great Gatsby*. This is what Faulkner says:

. . . the affirmation of a creed, the declaration of a faith, the postulation even of a very way of life: the loud strong voice that is America itself out of the soundless westward roar of the tremendous battered yet indomitably virgin continent where nothing save the vast unmoral sky limited what a man could try to do nor even the sky his success and its adulation if he just thought of the right twist to do it.

This is the Fitzgerald passage:

I became aware of the old island here that flowered once for Dutch sailors' eyes. . . . Gatsby believed in the green light, the orgastic future that year by year recedes before us. It eluded us then, but that's no matter — tomorrow we will run faster, stretch out our arms farther. . . . And one fine morning —
So we beat on, boats against the current, borne back ceaselessly into the past.

It is odd that Fitzgerald, identified with the American's capacity for magnificent expectations, should be the observer of the failure or at least partial defeat of those expectations and that Faulkner, the voice of cosmic pessimism, should assume (with a strange turn in the idiom: "if he just thought of the right twist to do it") the rhetorical optimism of Walt Whitman.

Faulkner, using an unnamed lawyer, who is suspiciously like Gavin Stevens, also takes a wry, and for the purposes of the story a gratuitous, look at Yankee capitalists: the "octopus of Wall Street and the millionaire owners of New England factories [who want] to erect once more the barricade of a Yankee tariff between the southern farmer and the hungry factories and cheap labor of the old world." And in another of the lawyer's speeches, a very dark cloud sweeps over the land bathed by American sunshine. Stevens foresees a series of horrible wars, with mechanical monsters filling the sky with "inflectionless uproar." But with the end of the final war man will remain, even though he will have lost his sense of continuity with the past, and his need to record history will have been forgotten. Still, for the most part, *Notes on a Horsethief* is a rhetorical blur of optimism.

Its action is this: An English groom steals a stallion which he races with great success through the Mississippi Valley region. The groom and the horse have an "affinity from heart to heart and glands to glands," and their flight is an "immortal pageant piece of the old deathless legend which was the crown and glory of man's own legend." He is accompanied by an unnamed elderly Negro, with equally noble motives, whose grandson or great-grandson rides the mythically fast and powerful stallion. The groom is not brought to trial, but if he had been, the lawyer would have defended him out of respect not for justice but for "man's serene and inalienable right to his folly," which right "the very American air exhale[s] for all earth's amazed and frantic envy." The old Negro is arrested and held in a small Missouri town, but the citizenry, out of a sense of justice that transcends the law, set him free.

Most of the rhetoric, and consequently the story itself, seems spurious and unreal. Good intentions are abundantly present, but the apostrophes to hope, to the future, and to man's unquenchable courage float too far above the concrete situation. We don't fully believe in the nameless groom or the old Negro because neither exists in terms of a complexity of motive or even as a physical image. Each is a suggestive blur, not a character. Certainly one does not accept the sentimental citizenry acting generously and in unison. It would be much easier to accept a mob acting in one accord. Figures in the story emerge tentatively, as though peering through the convolutions of the rhetorical sentences, but they are not seen or heard as people. In the earlier Faulkner, as well as in more recent short stories, the world and the people in it are seen in their own terms, even when they are lifted upward by the narrator's voice and to some extent merge into the flow of that voice. But situations and characters in *Notes on a Horsethief* have been made somnolent or have been hypnotized. The voice, almost, is all that is left. It presents its moralizing with a solemn, deliberate air. As speechmaking the story undoubtedly exists on a relatively high level. As fiction it seems a poor substitute for the earlier stories in which themes, situations, people were quickened and made to live, not effaced, by the narrator.

Since winning the Nobel Prize Faulkner has been away from Oxford more frequently than usual and has made a number of public appearances. During one trip, to the Kentucky Derby, he is said to have won a sizable amount of money for himself and the editors who entrusted their bets to his judgment. A part of the spring of 1951 he spent in Hollywood, another part in New York conferring about his play dealing with the redemption of Temple Drake. An acquaintance in New York ribbed Faulkner by saying that his not having frequented the theater, having seen only a handful of plays in twenty years, had not prevented his writing a play. "That's true," Faulkner replied, then added, "I don't read many novels either."

In April 1951 Faulkner was awarded the Ordre National de la Legion D'Honneur by the French consul in New Orleans. His acceptance speech was delivered in French, much to the surprise of his brother Murray, an FBI official, stationed in New Orleans, who himself had once lived in France.

During another 1951 trip away from Oxford, Faulkner received a telephone call from Jill, asking that he address her high school graduating class. Lonely and delighted to be talking with his daughter, he said he would give the address. So on May 28 Faulkner escorted his daughter and wife to the exercises at University High School and made the address.[4] Some members of the audience later said he could not be heard very well, but afterward Miss Ella Wright, who had been his teacher in grammar school, said to him: "William, you sounded as though you have been making speeches all your life." This is what Faulkner told the graduating seniors:

Years ago, before any of you were born, a wise Frenchman said, "If youth knew; if age could." We all know what he meant: that when you are young, you have the power to do anything, but you don't know what to do. Then, when you have got old and experience and observation have taught you answers, you are tired, frightened; you don't care, you want to be left alone as long as you yourself are safe; you no longer have the capacity or the will to grieve over any wrongs but your own.

So you young men and women in this room tonight, and in thousands of other rooms like this one about the earth today, have the power to change the world, rid it forever of war and injustice and suffering, provided you know how, know what to do. And so according to the old Frenchman, since you can't know what to do because you are young, then anyone standing here with a head full of white hair, should be able to tell you.

But maybe this one is not as old and wise as his white hairs pretend or claim. Because he can't give you a glib answer or pattern either. But he can tell you this, because he believes this. What threatens us today is fear. Not the atom bomb, nor even fear of it, because if the bomb fell on Oxford tonight, all it could do would be to kill us, which is nothing, since in doing that, it will have robbed itself of its only power over us: which is fear of it, the being afraid of it. Our danger is not that. Our danger is the forces of the world today which are trying to use man's fear to rob him of his individuality, his soul, trying to reduce him to an unthinking mass by fear and bribery — giving him free food which he has not earned, easy and valueless money which he has not worked for; — the economies or ideologies or political systems, communist or socialist or democratic, whatever they wish to call themselves, the tyrants and the politicians, American or European or Asiatic, whatever

The Right to Responsibility

they call themselves, who would reduce man to one obedient
mass for their own aggrandisement and power, or because they
themselves are baffled and afraid, afraid of, or incapable of, believing in man's capacity for courage and endurance and sacrifice.

That is what we must resist, if we are to change the world for
man's peace and security. It is not men in the mass who can and
will save Man. It is Man himself, created in the image of God so
that he shall have the power and the will to choose right from
wrong, and so be able to save himself because he is worth saving;
Man, the individual, man and woman, who will refuse always to
be tricked or frightened or bribed into surrendering, not just the
right but the duty too, to choose between justice and injustice,
courage and cowardice, sacrifice and greed, pity and self; — who
will believe always not only in the right of man to be free of injustice and rapacity and deception, but the duty and responsibility of man to see that justice and truth and pity and compassion
are done.

So, never be afraid. Never be afraid to raise your voice for honesty and truth and compassion, against injustice and lying and
greed. If you, not just you in this room tonight, but in all the thousands of other rooms like this one about the world today and
tomorrow and next week, will do this, not as a class or classes, but
as individuals, men and women, you will change the earth. In one
generation all the Napoleons and Hitlers and Caesars and Musso-
linis and Stalins and all the other tyrants who want power and
aggrandisement, and the simple politicians and timeservers who
themselves are merely baffled or ignorant or afraid, who have used,
or are using, or hope to use, man's fear and greed for man's en-
slavement, will have vanished from the face of it.

Requiem for a Nun,[5] published in the fall of 1951, is another
statement of affirmation. One clear idea that comes from the play,
which is a part of the book, is the need for purification through
suffering. "Just suffering. Not for anything; just suffering. Just because it is good for you." Temple confesses her offenses not to save
Nancy Mannigoe, but for the purification available through suffering: "We don't come here to save Nancy. What we came here
for is just to give Temple Drake a good fair honest chance to
suffer — just anguish for the sake of anguish." But there is much
else on the side of affirmation that is undefined. In the final scene,

157

The Tangled Fire of William Faulkner

Nancy tries to convert Temple to the ways of righteousness — but she isn't able to tell her what she should believe:

NANCY
(moving on after the Jailor)
Believe.

TEMPLE
Believe what, Nancy? Tell me.

NANCY
Believe.

The doctrine that Nancy has acted by and is to suffer death for at the hands of the state is the ancient one that the end justifies the means. Temple Drake, eight years after her *Sanctuary* experience, is married to Gowan Stevens, who has married her out of a desire to do the "right thing," and is uneasy in her domestic virtue. Nancy Mannigoe, dope fiend and whore (who has been "resurrected" after her death, as reported in *The Sound and the Fury*), is the nurse for Temple's baby and Temple's confidante. Into this Jefferson scene comes the brother of Red, Temple's lover from *Sanctuary*, who was despatched from life by Popeye's henchmen. The young man has found some of her letters to Red and is bent on blackmail. Temple, intrigued by the possibility of escape from virtue, offers to take her and Gowan's baby and run away with the young man. Nancy, to prevent this, kills the baby. The reader never gets beyond the horror of this violence. The act is monstrous — and thereafter all the talk, by Gavin and Gowan Stevens and the governor of Mississippi, about morality seems unintentionally ironical.

Requiem for a Nun is Faulkner's strangest book. The central situation in it is unbelievable, and its main character, Temple Drake, seems like a mannequin mouthing sentiments foreign to her porcelain-and-paper being. The structure of the story is no less strange. Temple's story is dramatized in three full acts, and printed in the form of a play, with the acts interlarded into long documentary accounts of the town of Jefferson, of the courthouse and the jail, and of Jackson, the state capital. Presumably the intention is to say, as a narrator says in an earlier book, "Yesterday today and tomorrow are Is," and also to say that Temple's story is involved in the history of Jefferson. But the device does not succeed, at least not very well, because the past of Jefferson, involved with events moral, immoral, and human, seems too foreign to the mannequin world of Temple.

But what of the historical chapters by themselves? They are eloquent and moving, as Faulkner can be when he is looking into the history of this region which has fed his imagination over the years. The past is caught as scene after scene and early settler after early settler move into focus in the flow from the past of a hundred years ago to the present of today. Many of Faulkner's earlier stories are recapitulated, sometimes in no more than a line or two. And the manner of telling the history is experimental: semicolons are used to link paragraph to paragraph, as the account flows on, and only at the end of each of the chapters is there a period. Seemingly Faulkner is not merely linking past and present, he is making both a simultaneous whole. Unfortunately *Requiem for a Nun* does not carry the conviction that Temple Drake is really concerned in the morality, the courage, the inviolable strength of Yoknapatawpha's settlers and their early descendants.

The failure or relative failure of *Requiem for a Nun* is not surprising, even for so great a writer as Faulkner. And a note from one writer in the *Saturday Review* may, if taken at face value, make one wonder whether another of Faulkner's works, his so-called *magnum opus*, will be on the level of some of his earlier work. Says the note: "William H. Faulkner is back once again on his Magnum Opus, which he's been writing for nearly twelve years. The manuscript — about 1,500 pages long already — has passed the half-million-word mark, and guesses about its ultimate length remain only guesses. I asked Saxe Commins, of Random House, what the book was about; his hand made a large sweeping gesture that was as telling as his reply: 'War and peace, the world, humanity.'"

——————————— 14

A Concluding View

THE FAULKNER CANON divides into three
periods, certain themes, techniques, and mannerisms being common to all of them. *Soldiers' Pay, Mosquitoes,* and some of the
stories in *These Thirteen* possess many of the characteristics of
late nineteenth-century literature: the Keatsian rhetoric modified
by Tennyson into something more wan, abstract, more hopelessly
sad, a divine despair, and the tiredness of an earth that knows all
defeats; Swinburne's eroticism, that is more of sound, color, and
mist than of the flesh; and the arty elegance of the *Yellow Book,*
language willing to imitate the stylized gesture of the artifact, and
an ennui that is at once young and old as the first satyr. Faulkner
has never belonged to the school of "a pure American prose" — he
is an artist and rhetorician, a willing ally of language.

To the second period, when Faulkner really finds himself as an
artist, belong *The Sound and the Fury, As I Lay Dying, Sanctuary,
Light in August, Doctor Martino and Other Stories, Pylon,
Absalom, Absalom!, The Unvanquished,* and *The Wild Palms.*
Generally these are stories of terrifying violence, exacerbated
humor, and grim dignity. The horrors are steadily kept in the foreground and sometimes a thin margin of victory is allowed a protagonist. In many, but not all of these volumes, Faulkner exploits
his own region, and in almost all of them he experiments endlessly

A Concluding View

with methods of narration — drawing the reader into and through the involutions of page-long sentences and forcing him to hold in mind details and phrases that are meaningful only at the end, when the whole context of a story lives brilliantly, with fact illumining fact.

No two stories, however, are told in quite the same way. In *The Sound and the Fury* the consciousness of three characters is revealed as though the reader lived successively in each mind — and then the range of consciousness broadens, enlarging its focus, until a history of the whole action becomes clear. In *As I Lay Dying* each character develops, through his own awareness, his relationship to the symbolic, yet painfully realistic, funeral journey from the Bundren farm to Jefferson. Most of the remaining stories are episodic, but each has its special devices: the Gothic framework of *Absalom, Absalom!*, the double plot and analogous actions of *Light in August*, the foreshortened (to use James' term) action of *Pylon*, the sequence of related short stories in *The Unvanquished*, and the merely thematic relationship of the alternated sections of *The Wild Palms*. *Sanctuary* is not nearly so experimental in structure, but, through its careful imagery and symbolism, it suggests the conventions of a highly stylized play. These novels make evident Faulkner's indebtedness to the tradition of the modern novel — and equally evident his contributions to that tradition. Not least among these contributions is the way in which his language, repeatedly, seems of a piece with his subject, evoking it in its own terms, then rising on itself as a choral voice, Faulkner's own characteristic idiom, taut, connotative, richly rhetorical, and hypnotic.

In the third period, beginning with *The Hamlet*, Faulkner offers some hope for the human condition, a promise of release. The hope is explored in *Go Down Moses*, most significantly in "The Bear" and "Delta Autumn." In *Intruder in the Dust, Knight's Gambit*, and *Requiem for a Nun* there are various attempts to elevate political programs and sermons into the self-sufficient, isolated entities of art forms. In *Go Down Moses* there is some of Faulkner's most brilliant and sustained rhetoric. In *Intruder in the Dust* and in *Knight's Gambit* there is a merging of detective story deductions and regional sociological themes. And *Requiem for a Nun* combines a play and history, interlarding acts between chapters of historical recollections and musings, and suggesting thereby the judgments the past makes on the actions of Temple Drake, the "heroine."

These three periods suggest the variety of attitudes and of themes to be found in Faulkner's work, some of which overlap or merge in a way that discourages neat schemata. From Victorian and *fin de siècle* literature Faulkner borrowed a sense of everything in decay. The created worlds of *Soldiers' Pay, Sartoris, Mosquitoes, The Sound and the Fury*, and *Sanctuary* participate in this vision of things. Superimposed, or, better, imbedded in the historical matrix of this nineteenth-century world is the modern wasteland — men in search of self-definition, despairing of meaning, or wantonly giving themselves to lives of amoral violence. Occasionally, as in *Pylon* and certain of the short stories about World War I, the wasteland is peculiarly of this century, largely free from its origins or connections with the last century.

As I Lay Dying and *The Wild Palms* define some of the means leading to significant actions: living in a harsh physical world one must violate one's aloneness, one must be committed to a life of the spirit, willing to suffer indignities and pain to achieve a margin of self-respect.

Through several of the books, either as major or minor themes, runs Faulkner's intense dislike of the repressions caused by the rigid mind. *Light in August* presents outrages done and violences caused by the literal-minded pietists grimly serving patriotism or religion. *Absalom, Absalom!* may also be read as a story of violence caused by a rigidity of spirit. Both "A Rose for Emily" and *Miss Zilphia Gant*, somewhat similarly but each in its own specialized Freudian milieu, are also stories of repressive rules giving rise to violence. *The Unvanquished* may be read as Faulkner's critique of a stereotyped code of manners which lead to cruelties and injustices.

The Hamlet is a folk comedy, making ample use of the tall tale

A Concluding View

and farcical actions; and though much of the book is bitter, the central intention is comedy in the old sense: man survives his own greed, inanities, foolishness, and stupidities. There are wonderfully funny scenes in many of Faulkner's books but *The Hamlet* is the only novel, with the very doubtful exception of *Sanctuary*, that is comic in intention and in theme.

All the latest books suggest ways of ameliorating harsh situations. *Go Down Moses* asks the reader to contemplate on the one hand the mistreatment of the Negro and on the other the clean and purifying spirit of a wilderness that preceded civilization and its ills. *Intruder in the Dust* offers a solution to the Negro problem, allowing the collective southern conscience to ease itself of its guilt, and not allowing virtue to be forced upon it by the federal government. *Knight's Gambit*, through a collection of detective stories, is filled with sententious asides, and *Requiem for a Nun* asserts the need for faith in the eternal virtues of love and fidelity.

In reply to a question once put to Faulkner by one of his interviewers, he said he had read very little in the historical studies of the Civil War, or of the South generally. What he knows of or believes about his region's history he knows by word of mouth, by having assimilated some notions and prejudices and resisted others. Considering that Faulkner is commonly looked upon as the "historian" of Yoknapatawpha County, his stories of the nineteenth century are not relatively numerous: in addition to several Chickasaw stories there are only *Absalom, Absalom!*, *The Unvanquished*, and parts of *Go Down Moses*. *The Hamlet* has a horse-and-buggy, pre-World War I setting, but the bulk of Faulkner's stories are from the 1920s and later. If he is to be thought of as a historian it should be as a historian primarily of his own century, but such a designation is neither more nor less appropriate for him than for most other novelists. As a writer of fiction, he has taken his subjects and themes where he could find them: among the country people, barn-storming pilots, the Negroes, sailors, an Italian priest, a local barber. That he has made scenes from the Civil War and parts of southern life live so luminously that certain readers think

The Tangled Fire of William Faulkner

of him primarily as a historian is a compliment to his genius for creating a sense of life. The capacity to create a sense of life in great variety is extremely rare, and Faulkner's having it is a most important element in his position and stature as a writer.

Like many another American novelist, Faulkner has worked in isolation, away from fellow writers, who might have helped him to be more knowledgeable. But in his isolation he has been free to work out his successful experiments, just as he has been free, or obliged, to look searchingly at the fields and lawns and shacks and plantation houses and at the men and women of his own region.

It is true that Faulkner was a part of the New Orleans literary world at a period when the modern esthetic was in process of crystallization, and that for many years he was a close student of fiction. But it is also true that, in one sense, Faulkner is not an intellectual. His claiming to be a "writer, not a literary man" — the American novelist's tradition that abstract speculations should be foreign to him — is only partly a pose. Faulkner is probably much more deserving of the phrase "untutored genius" than was Shakespeare, product of a strict Latin-school education. Faulkner appears to have native shrewdness rather than the wide knowledge that makes possible unerring taste and judgment. Obviously that shrewdness is at times not enough — but Faulkner's limitations have not kept him from becoming, far and away, the best American novelist in the first half of the twentieth century.[1]

When Faulkner was twenty-eight years old and just beginning to write fiction, Sherwood Anderson warned him that he had almost too much talent, that it might use him and prevent his development. That Faulkner did not allow this to happen is now quite clear. A writer's contemporaries are frequently mistaken, or so posterity feels, in the men they single out for acclaim. Faulkner's contemporaries have been a little slow to place him in the line of greatness, even in the relatively thin and narrow American line of greatness, which suggests that they had first to learn in what ways he has been an original, and, having learned that, to discover in what ways he has used that originality to quicken the permanent truths. Genius being rare, we may assume that posterity will neither forget nor neglect him.

Notes and Index

NOTES

Chapter 1. The Sartorises of Jefferson

[1] For this and other information about Faulkner's childhood, see Bill Hudson, "Faulkner before Sanctuary," *Carolina Magazine*, 69 (April 1935), 11–14.

[2] The general history of the Falkner family is provided in Phil Stone, "William Faulkner: The Man and His Work," *Oxford Magazine*, vol. 1 (1934), nos. 1, 2, and 3. For an excellent account of Colonel Falkner, see Robert Cantwell, "The Faulkners," *New World Writing*, 1952.

[3] James Kemble Vardaman (1861–1930) was both governor of Mississippi and U.S. senator, one of President Wilson's "wilful men." In Mississippi, thanks to the changed primary law, he campaigned dramatically and successfully by stressing class lines. He also appealed to the tenant class by telling them that the education of Negroes would endanger their own political domination; and he was accused of extending the spoils system. However, he did attack the practice of leasing state convicts to private corporations and persons. At many stages during his career he was the idol of many Mississippi voters.

[4] The following provide a fairly detailed history of Oxford and Lafayette County: Federal Writers' Project, *Mississippi: A Guide to the Magnolia State* (New York, 1938); J. C. Hathorn, "A Period Study of Lafayette County from 1836 to 1860," master's thesis, University of Mississippi, 1930; Minnie Smith Holt, "Oxford, Mississippi," master's thesis, University of Mississippi, 1936; P. L. Rainwater, "When Major General Grant Was in Oxford," *Oxford Magazine*, 1 (1934), 3–4; Medford Evans, "Oxford, Mississippi," *Southwest Review*, 15 (Autumn 1929), 46–63.

[5] Phil Stone, *op. cit.*

[6] There is considerable disagreement among Faulkner's acquaintances about his evaluation of himself and of his work. When asked, for example, by a student at the University of Mississippi to rank himself among the five leading American novelists, Faulkner replied: "Thomas Wolfe: he had much courage and wrote as if he didn't have long to live; William Faulkner; Dos Passos; Ernest Hemingway: he has no courage, has never crawled out on a limb. He has never been known to use a word that might cause the reader to check with a dictionary to see if it is properly used; John Steinbeck: at one time

The Tangled Fire of William Faulkner

I had great hopes for him — now I don't know." (Lavon Rascoe, "An Interview with William Faulkner," *Western Review*, 15 [Summer 1951], 300–304.) The difficulty in commenting on his hierarchy of American writers is that while in one sense his placing himself second seems arrogant, in another sense it seems humble, because quite obviously he is a much greater writer than Wolfe.

Faulkner's younger brother John has said: "I think Bill is the greatest writer that's ever lived, including Shakespeare. A few years ago Bill told me he was goin' to win the Nobel prize. He wasn't braggin' — he just knows he's the best writer of them all." Brother John undoubtedly indulged in a little exaggeration here, but he may well be right in saying that Faulkner is better than any of his immediate contemporaries. But this family assurance, however well based in fact, can sometimes sound a little arrogant and pretentious. To take an instance: One of Faulkner's friends, who had been unsuccessful in getting a publisher, spoke to him about his problem and was asked, "How about writing for the pulps?" The friend, slightly offended, said, "Well, my stuff may not be very good, but it has some quality and that would prevent its being acceptable to pulp editors. Could you write for the pulps?" And Faulkner, not hesitating, is said to have responded, "Why, of course, I could write anything." "That," his friend is said to have retorted, "is because you are a ——— ——— Falkner."

Some of Faulkner's acquaintances tend to explain such stories in terms of Faulkner's shyness. Nunnally Johnson, for whom Faulkner has worked in Hollywood, says he is extremely shy and that he usually needed a few drinks to relax sufficiently to collaborate in writing a script.

In Phil Stone's view, Faulkner is devoid equally of conceit and humility. All of his friends, however, insist that Faulkner's generosity and integrity are close to being absolute. Early in the 1930s, when Stone was in financial difficulties, Faulkner sold some of his property to help his friend. Years later, when Faulkner received the Nobel Prize, Stone said: "A lot of us talk about decency, about honor, about loyalty, about gratitude. Bill doesn't talk about these things: he lives them." (*Oxford Eagle*, November 16, 1950, p. 3.) Harvey Breit, a friend of Faulkner's, has also insisted on the sense one receives of Faulkner's absolute honesty. ("A Sense of Faulkner," *Partisan Review*, 18 [January 1951], 88–94.)

There is an interesting sketch of Faulkner in Oxford, seen through the eyes of Phil Stone, published in the *Oxford Magazine* in 1934: Stone goes out of his way to insist on the nonlegendary qualities and characteristics of the man, "who is the sanest and the most wholesome person I have ever known, but who is at times and in some small ways . . . the most aggravating, damned human being on this earth."

Arthur Palmer Hudson, the folklorist, and later professor of English at the University of North Carolina, was frequently the golfing companion of Stone and Faulkner. He remembers Faulkner as a fine golfer, a good companion, a man possessed with a highly developed sense of humor who could be vivacious in his talk or quiet and withdrawn.

Chapter 2. Period of Apprenticeship

[1] *New Republic*, August 6, 1919.
[2] See Arthur Wigfall Green, "William Faulkner at Home," *Sewanee Review*, 40 (Summer 1932), 294–306.

Notes

[3] Marshal Smith, "Faulkner of Mississippi," *Bookman*, 74 (December 1931), 411–417.

[4] Stark Young, "New Year's Craw," *New Republic*, 93 (January 12, 1938), 283–284.

[5] Bill Hudson, "Faulkner before Sanctuary," *Carolina Magazine*, 69 (April 1935), 11–14.

[6] Robert W. Daniel, *A Catalogue of the Writings of William Faulkner* (New Haven: Yale University Library, 1942), p. 7.

[7] Pelican Bookshop, 1926.

[8] *Time*, April 7, 1941, p. 98.

[9] *Dial*, 78 (April 1925), 269–279.

[10] Milwaukee: Casanova Press, 1932.

[11] Published in the *Double Dealer*; reprinted in *Salmagundi*.

[12] The series appeared as follows: "Mirrors of Chartres Street," February 8, 1925, pp. 1 and 6; "Damon and Pythias Unlimited," February 15, 1925, p. 7; "Home," February 22, 1925, p. 3; "Cheest," April 5, 1925, p. 4; "Out of Nazareth," April 12, 1925, p. 4; "The Kingdom of God," April 26, 1925, p. 4; "The Rosary," May 3, 1925, p. 2; "The Cobbler," May 10, 1925, p. 7; "Chance," May 17, 1925, p. 7; "Sunset," May 24, 1925, p. 4; "The Kid Learns," May 31, 1925, p. 2. "Out of Nazareth" was illustrated by William Spratling.

[13] *Atlantic Monthly*, 191 (June 1953), pp. 27–29.

[14] F. L. Gwynn, in "Faulkner's Prufrock — and Other Observations," *J.E.G.P.*, vol. 52 (January 1953), feels that the characters in *Mosquitoes* suggest the world of Prufrock.

Chapter 3. Emergence of a Major Writer

[1] Lavon Rascoe, "An Interview with William Faulkner," *Western Review*, 15 (Summer 1951), 300–304.

[2] Malcolm Cowley (ed.), *The Portable Faulkner* (New York: Viking Press, 1946).

[3] An article by Sumner Powell, "William Faulkner Celebrates Easter, 1928," *Perspective*, 2 (Summer 1949), 195–218, emphasizes (perhaps over-emphasizes) the Christian symbolism in *The Sound and the Fury*. The pre-occupation with Christianity has not, I think, been given the stress it deserves by Faulkner critics. In the chapter on *Light in August* (6) I attempt to show how important it is.

[4] See, for example, the discussion between Stephen and Lynch in chapter V of *A Portrait of the Artist*.

[5] "Writing Right Smart Fun, Says Faulkner," *Dallas Morning News*, February 14, 1932, IV, 2.

[6] Evelyn Scott, *On William Faulkner's The Sound and the Fury* (New York: Jonathan Cape and Harrison Smith, 1929).

[7] During Faulkner's first years back in Oxford he supported himself by doing odd jobs. He painted advertising signs all over Lafayette County. And he worked for a hundred dollars a month as a furnace tender at the town power plant. Sometimes he sat by the hot water drain writing poetry about brooks dancing gaily between violet-covered banks.

On June 20, 1929, he married Estelle Oldham Franklin, a divorcée. She had been a childhood sweetheart, but she had married someone else, a cotton broker, and gone elsewhere to live. Before his marriage Faulkner had won

The Tangled Fire of William Faulkner

the affection of Victoria and Malcolm, Mrs. Franklin's two children. He took them on picnics, met them as they left school, and entertained them with stories. When Malcolm heard his mother had married his friend, he visited different neighbors on South Street to tell them: "Mama and Mr. Bill are married."

Faulkner seems not to have been so friendly with Oxonians in general. Medford Evans, who that summer was doing a brief historical sketch of Oxford, reported on the town's view of their young novelist: "His fellow-townsmen make no pretense of being able to understand him. He is one of the most talked-about and most seldom talked-to persons in the community. He walks a great deal by himself, carries a cane, and wears a moustache, though to be sure, these habits cannot be vouched for as still characteristic since he married this summer. He is said to be temperamental even with his friends, being at times a ready talker and again incommunicative." (Medford Evans, "Oxford, Mississippi," *Southwest Review*, 15 [Autumn 1929], 46–63.)

⁸ For a highly detailed and useful account of *As I Lay Dying*, see Olga Vickery's article in *William Faulkner: Two Decades of Criticism*, eds. F. J. Hoffman and Olga W. Vickery (Michigan State College Press, 1951), pp. 189–205.

Chapter 4. *Sanctuary* and Popular Success

¹ 7 (March 21, 1931), 673–674.

² "The Private World of William Faulkner," *'48 the Magazine of the Year*, 2 (May 1948), 83–94.

³ *Saturday Review of Literature*, 11 (October 20, 1934), 217.

⁴ Timothy Fuller, "The Story of Jack and Jill," 15 (December 19, 1936), 10.

⁵ Carvel Collins, "A Note on *Sanctuary*," *Harvard Advocate*, 135 (November 1951), 16.

⁶ An interesting interpretation of *Sanctuary* is Wyndham Lewis' "Moralist with a Corncob," *Men without Art* (Cassell and Co., 1934), in which the emphasis is on the satirical elements which are strongly although probably not centrally present. The essence of the novel, Lewis says, "is to be sought for in the pessimism engendered in any American of intelligence by the spectacle of child corruption conjoined and coeval with the fantastic lawlessness which came in with Prohibition, culminating in the notorious case of the Lindberg Baby, and which gave Popeye and his kind (the violent little gutter-Caesars of the Underworld) their chance. For it is not an accident that William Faulkner's gangster is one of the most insignificant and useless of men, brought to the top by the growing chaos in the heart of society — for whom human beings are flies to be dismissed from life as lightly as a troublesome insect, for the reason that he is himself a thing of the same order — that is undoubtedly the idea, and a highly moral one, you will agree."

Another interesting, but probably confused, interpretation is Lawrence Kubie's "William Faulkner's *Sanctuary*: An Analysis," *Saturday Review of Literature*, 11 (October 20, 1934), 218ff. Kubie says that the novel "represents the working out in phantasy of the problems of impotence in men, meaning by impotence a frailty in all spheres of institutional striving. In the end, however, this impotence always is seen to have a direct relation to psycholo-sexual potency. It is as though a sophisticated and civilized man is conducting a constant struggle which seems to have in it three direct objects of fear, a fear of women, a fear of other men, and a fear of the community

Notes

and of society in general. All of these three fears are dramatized in this story." Kubie never makes quite clear whether he is writing about Faulkner's phantasies or generalizing, like Lewis, about the state of men in the modern world.

See also Peter Lisca, "Some New Light on Faulkner's *Sanctuary*," *Faulkner Studies*, 2 (Spring 1953), 5–9, an article which holds that family coercion caused Temple to testify against Goodwin.

Chapter 5. *These Thirteen*, and Other Stories

[1] "Beyond the Talking," 57 (May 20, 1931), 23–24.

[2] New York: Jonathan Cape and Harrison Smith, 1931. Centaur Library of Chatto and Windus, London, issued it the following year. In 1939 it was published in a French translation by Gallimard, Paris.

[3] "Books," *Herald Tribune*, 8, November 8, 1931, 1ff.

[4] "Ad Astra," "Red Leaves," "A Rose for Emily," and "Dry September" had been published. Magazines and dates of publication for Faulkner's stories prior to 1942 are listed in *A Catalogue of the Writings of William Faulkner*, by Robert Daniel.

[5] There is, or there at least seems to be, a strong echo of the folk character Sam Slick in this highly charged rhetoric Faulkner has written about his aspirations as a writer. One of the broadsides about Sam Slick, the Yankee peddler, published in London, contains this passage: "We Yankees don't do things like you Britishers; we are born in a hurry, educated at full speed, our spirit is at high pressure, and our life resembles a shooting star, till death surprises us like an electric shock. . . . I am Sam Slick the Yankee peddler — I can ride on a flash of lightning and catch a thunderbolt in my fist. . . ." Since it is quite clear that Faulkner has used folk stories and tall tales in *Mosquitoes*, *The Hamlet*, and "The Bear," usually transmuting them for his own ends, there seems no good reason for not recognizing the folk element which appears to be a part of the original inspiration of this passage. (Sam Slick is discussed in *American Humor* by Constance Rourke [Harcourt, Brace, 1931], chap. II.)

[6] Dallas, Texas, 1932.

Arranging for the publication of *Miss Zilphia Gant* caused Henry Nash Smith to visit Faulkner in Oxford in January 1932. The impressions he gained of Faulkner were quite different from those which Faulkner made upon the visitors at the University of Virginia the preceding year. As Smith and Faulkner sat and talked, before a coal fire in the ante-bellum house into which the Faulkners had recently moved, Faulkner stroked a cat named Bit. "I raised this cat from a kitten," he said. "Her mother went off and left her and I fed her with a rag soaked in milk." He talked about the plans he and Mrs. Faulkner had for fixing up the house, and he joked about how hard it was to get any work out of their two Negro servants, who were in love. "They stand for hours, one with a mop, the other with a broom, looking into each other's eyes." He said he preferred the Oxford he had known as a boy to the newer Oxford of billboards and autos.

Smith asked Faulkner about the source of the episode in which Doom, the Indian chief, has his slaves drag a houseboat twelve miles inland for his use as a residence (it is in "Red Leaves") and was told that the incident had been invented. Talking about local types, Faulkner said, "There is no violent contrast between hill country and bottom land in this section, but I can tell hill

171

The Tangled Fire of William Faulkner

folks from bottom folks by meeting them on the street. The hill women hold their heads high and stride out from the hips. The women from the bottom look like dried up cows that don't earn their keep." (Henry Nash Smith, "Writing Right Smart Fun, Says Faulkner," *Dallas Morning News*, February 14, 1932, IV, 2.)

During his visit Smith had occasion to see Faulkner at work in his study, where he worked from an early hour until mid or late morning. Faulkner sat almost primly at his desk, writing with a fountain pen, later transcribing the whole novel on the typewriter. Two stacks of paper were in perfect alignment on the desk. Each sheet had finely penciled margins in which revisions were to be made. Faulkner wrote across each sheet in lines as straight as a draftsman's and in a minuscule, almost cryptic hand. When a page was filled it was placed face down on the second stack. Finished manuscripts, like *As I Lay Dying*, had been neatly bound in cardboard with librarian's tape. Faulkner, it could be, has not merely the obsessive, perfectionist character common to many writers, but the excessiveness of a man who contains himself by imposing severe restrictions.

Chapter 6. A Part of the Southern Mores: Protestantism

[1] Modern Library edition, 1950, see pages 61, 68, 77–78, 340–343, and 406.
[2] *American Mercury*, 36 (October 1935), 156–168. Reprinted in *Collected Stories*, 1950.

Chapter 7. The Folklore of Speed

[1] Boston: Four Seas Co., 1924, with preface by Stone.
[2] Harrison Smith and Robert Haas, 1934.
[3] Harrison Smith and Robert Haas, 1934.
[4] In *Collected Stories* four Ikkemotube stories appear under the heading "The Wilderness": "Red Leaves," "A Justice," "A Courtship," and "Lo!" One Greenwood Lefore (see *Requiem for a Nun*, p. 106) may have suggested the character of Saucier Weddell.
[5] Harrison Smith and Robert Haas, 1935.
[6] John, whose physical resemblance to William is marked, has had a varied career. He ran away from home and enlisted, under age, in the army, and was brought back home by his father; he worked as an engineer after studying at the University of Mississippi; he managed his brother's farm; he wrote *Men Working* (about the WPA) and *Dollar Cotton*; and now he teaches writing at the university.
Dean, for whom the local airport is named, was killed in Pontotoc County, apparently after a student flier "froze" at the controls. Dean had graduated from the university and was working out of the Memphis airport. His marker in the family plot reads August 15, 1907–November 10, 1935.
[7] "Folklore of the Air," *American Mercury*, 36 (November 1935), 370–372.

Chapter 8. Consequences of the Old Order

[1] *The World of William Faulkner* (Duke University Press, 1952).
[2] Clifton Fadiman, for example, discussed it as "Anti-Narrative, a set of complex devices used to keep the story from being told . . . as if a child were to go to work on it with a pair of shears." (*New Yorker*, 12 [October 31, 1936], 63.)

Notes

Subsequent criticism has frequently considered *Absalom, Absalom!* as the greatest of Faulkner's novels. Perspective has made it possible to see that the fervor and violence are under control, that the shadowy, mysterious landscape evokes a religious awe, that behind the anguish is compassion. The terror of human existence is seen in the novel. These characteristics, which in sum are called expressionism, seem readily analyzable — but the reviewers of the novel, in the very middle of our most political decade, seemed not to know what to make of it. Even a sympathetic critic, like William Troy, was fairly sure that the manner of the narration was a mistake.

Random House published *Absalom, Absalom!* (1936) in an edition of about ten thousand copies. Two editions were brought out in England, but the American edition was quite sufficient for the demand until after Faulkner received the Nobel Prize, after which it was brought out in Modern Library.

That Faulkner's financial situation was not as good as it might have been and that he felt harassed is suggested by the appearance of this advertisement in the Memphis *Commercial Appeal* in the summer of 1936: "I will not be responsible for any bills made or debts contracted or notes or checks signed by Mrs. William Faulkner or Mrs. Estelle Oldham Faulkner — William Faulkner, Oxford, Miss." Reporters, expecting to find the Faulkner marriage breaking up, descended on Oxford, but they found him helping his wife stage a birthday party for their three-year-old daughter. Faulkner explained: "It's just a matter of protection until I pay up my back debts." Invited by Twentieth Century Fox, Faulkner went to Hollywood, to work on *Slave Ship*, another of the stories for which his special quality was needed.

³ *The Unvanquished* (Random House, 1938). Many of the characters from *The Unvanquished* appear also in "My Grandmother Millard and General Bedford Forrest and the Battle of Harrykin Creek," *Collected Stories* (1950), pp. 667–699.

⁴ In a review of *William Faulkner: Two Decades of Criticism, Sewanee Review* (Winter 1952), I have attempted to point out what I think are mistaken emphases in the critical approaches that make Faulkner a "historian" of his region.

⁵ *Specimens of Mississippi Folk-Lore* (Mississippi Folk-Lore Society, 1928).

Chapter 9. Two Types of Love

¹ Once asked by an interviewer whether her husband had ever seemed embittered by the long years of local indifference to his work or by the frequently unfavorable reviews he had received, Mrs. Faulkner said, "Not at all. That's what makes him great. He is personally indifferent to what people think of him. He never reads any reviews of his books and he's never been bothered by the fact that Oxford has been totally unaware of his greatness as a writer."

Generally, it probably is true that Faulkner tried not to be hurt by the indifference and misunderstanding, but on at least one occasion he responded touchily to a suggestion that he was not widely read. In the '30s Dan Brennan, now the author of two novels but then of college age and an aspiring writer, visited Oxford unannounced. He phoned the evening of his arrival and explained the nature of his pilgrimage to Mrs. Faulkner, and, after a long pause, to Faulkner himself, who told Brennan that they had some difficulties with visitors but that he should come out to their house the next morning.

The next day, the young admirer found Faulkner walking in the yard. His

The Tangled Fire of William Faulkner

greeting was courteous and kind even though, as Brennan soon discovered, his host had been suffering all week from insomnia — "like an electric light burning in my head and refusing to be put out." When Brennan, under a misapprehension, said Faulkner had been at a movie the night before, the air chilled suddenly — No sir, he had not been at a movie. There were other Falkners in town; must have been one of them.

Brennan remembers Mrs. Faulkner as a fine-looking woman, not especially interested in books except as they were a part of her husband's career, and complementary to the taciturnity and reserve of her husband.

After lunch Faulkner retired to his study to read the journal that Brennan had been keeping. The writing, he said, upon rejoining Brennan, was promising, but he had one criticism: in describing a person the writer should be sure he renders him sharply and clearly. They then piled into the 1936 Ford touring car, and after stopping briefly at Faulkner's mother's house, went for a picnic. During the afternoon Faulkner spent most of the time playing with his daughter Jill.

After dinner, the Faulkners and Brennan sat together in the living room. Finding Faulkner withdrawn and quiet — "He can sit there forever without saying anything!" — Brennan was betrayed into an inept remark. He had been unable to buy *Sartoris* in a Minneapolis bookstore — a clerk there claimed never to have heard of it. Why weren't Mr. Faulkner's books more available? Faulkner stared at him, then replied with no little ice in his voice that his books were available in *all* bookstores. What was Brennan trying to imply? Mrs. Faulkner said, "Now Will, he didn't mean it that way." Brennan said Mrs. Faulkner was right, he meant no offense. During the remainder of the evening there was an obvious effort to repair the situation, but Brennan upon leaving did not feel his visit had been a success. Some weeks later, back in Minneapolis, he was surprised to receive a friendly note from Mrs. Faulkner saying Will and she had enjoyed his visit very much and hoped he would return.

² Random House, 1939.

³ The writer who did that interview with Faulkner and who wrote the review for *Time* was Robert Cantwell, and in "The Faulkners: Recollections of a Gifted Family," *New World Writing* (The New American Library, 1952), pp. 300–315, he has recalled some of his impressions of Faulkner and gone on into a further account of him. Over and above the value of his impressions of Faulkner in his family setting there is an interesting account of Faulkner's attitude toward his great-grandfather, and Cantwell has reconstructed Colonel Falkner's life.

William Faulkner indicated to Cantwell that he thought his great-grandfather was probably a very arrogant and conceited man who had "to be a big dog." But Cantwell's research suggests that the man himself, unlike the Colonel Sartoris of the fiction, lived to a great extent in direct opposition to an extravagant and artificial code that invited dueling over small or imagined affronts. Cantwell shows conclusively that the great-grandfather demonstrated patience and restraint in refusing to take part in a series of duels which he knew to have no justification, and finally gave his life when he refused to fight with J. H. Thurmond, his former partner and the man he had defeated for a seat in the legislature.

Faulkner introduced Cantwell to Uncle Ned, an aged Negro who had been Colonel Falkner's body servant and had cared for three generations of the Falkner family. (It has been suggested, although not by Cantwell, that this old man was the basis for Lucas Beauchamp.)

Notes

Faulkner told Cantwell that he had read almost no history of the Civil War, that he heard what he knew from the mouths of the old men, and he told him that he had grown up with a Negro boy like Ringo in *The Unvanquished*.

⁴ Lavon Rascoe, "An Interview with William Faulkner," *Western Review*, 15 (Summer 1951), 300–304. Irving Howe in *William Faulkner, A Critical Study* (Random House, 1952), has worked out a number of thematic parallels between the two stories.

Presumably the two stories are intended to be read as having a simultaneous existence — the alternating chapters would suggest this. The flood, however, is in 1927, during Herbert Hoover's administration, but Charles Wilbourne is shown looking for a WPA job, which of course had to be during F. D. Roosevelt's administration, beginning in 1932.

Chapter 10. Frenchman's Bend and the Folk Tradition

¹ In the summer of 1940 Dan Brennan accepted the invitation extended by Mrs. Faulkner and returned to Oxford for a week's visit. Faulkner took Brennan with him on visits to his farm, occasionally indulging in literary talk. Was there, Brennan asked him, an actual village like Frenchman's Bend? No, no actual village, but there was an area he had in mind, and had Brennan noticed that one sometimes saw a huge fireplace, obviously from an old plantation house that had disappeared, with a nigger shanty built up to it? That sort of thing would be in his new book, the one about the Snopes family. . . . Did Faulkner feel his fiction was getting better year by year? No, he did not. Ten years earlier he had been more inclined to experiment than he was now. After a time a man writes himself out. He has only so many good stories in him. Nor did he feel like doing much reading these days. Yes, he would give Brennan a list of books a young writer might study with profit. Well, first, the great novel of our time would be *Buddenbrooks*. He would also list Shakespeare's *Sonnets* and *Henry V*, something from Dickens, and certainly Conrad's *Lord Jim* and *Nostromo*, and . . . Was he, Faulkner, Bayard Sartoris? Of course not, he was not any of his characters! Are there good women novelists? Well, Evelyn Scott was pretty good, for a woman. . . .

Brennan's understanding of Faulkner, as it was formed that week, included an extended sense of what he had felt during his earlier visit. Faulkner could be extremely withdrawn, but he was also alert and self-contained. In build the man was delicate, very small-boned, and in appearance, not in manner, almost effeminate. The face was saturnine, with intensely black eyes, like a gambler's, twinkling or glinting fire, a hooked nose and prematurely gray hair that contrasted with his dark mustache. His manner was polite, kind, professorial, not quite a Hollywood caricature of the professor but none the less one-dimensional, solemn, preoccupied and a little sententious. . . .

One afternoon Brennan read in the study while Faulkner worked on some of the stories that were to appear in *Go Down Moses*. The study itself was lined with books, many of them novels from the 1920s. After putting some final touches to "Go Down Moses" Faulkner told Brennan he much admired the title, and together they went outside where Faulkner read the story to Jill. Asked whether she liked it, Jill replied, "Daddy, it is too sad." Faulkner told Brennan the story or the idea for it occurred to him after he had seen a coffin with an Oxford address resting in the local depot. . . . After another

175

The Tangled Fire of William Faulkner

session in the library Brennan asked for and was given some of the discarded sheets with which Faulkner had been working. The sheets, which indicate that he was working at two stories simultaneously, and that he made lengthy and painstaking revisions, were inscribed, "To Dan Brennan. William Faulkner. July 19, 1940. Oxford, Miss."

[2] *Specimens of Mississippi Folk-Lore* (Mississippi Folk-Lore Society, 1928), p. v.

[3] H. M. Campbell and R. E. Foster, in *William Faulkner* (University of Oklahoma Press, 1951), say that Phil Stone, to whom *The Hamlet* is dedicated, "maintains that he and Faulkner worked up the Snopes saga together in a spirit of anecdotal whimsy. Models were at hand in and around Oxford." Faulkner told Malcolm Cowley that he plans two or three volumes on the Snopes family, and the authors of *William Faulkner* say that new characters will be Admiral Dewey Snopes, Montgomery Ward Snopes, and Dollar Watch Snopes.

The first story written for the saga was "Spotted Horses," *Scribner's* (June 1931), then "The Hound," *Harper's* (August 1931), and "Lizzards in Jamshyd's Courtyard," *Saturday Evening Post* (February 27, 1932). "I wrote them," Faulkner said, "mainly because 'Spotted Horses' had created a character named Suratt. Later a man of that name turned up at home, so I changed my man to Ratliff. . . ." The first two stories appeared in *Dr. Martino and Other Stories*, then, with "Lizzards in Jamshyd's Courtyard," they were greatly expanded to suit the story line in *The Hamlet*. The murderer in "The Hound" was originally called Cotten, but for *The Hamlet* he becomes Mink Snopes, and, one should add, the detail in the later version of "Spotted Horses" is much more brilliant than that in the early version.

[4] *Harper's*, 179 (June 1939), 86–96. Reprinted in *Collected Stories*.

[5] A. B. Longstreet was president of the University of Mississippi from 1849 to 1856. It is obvious that Faulkner knows his *Georgia Scenes*, as would almost any literate southerner of his generation.

[6] Virginia Boyle, *Devil Tales* (Harper, 1900).

[7] For the record: Professor Arthur Palmer Hudson, in reply to a question from me, has said, "I am reasonably sure that Mr. Faulkner was acquainted in a general way with the work I was doing in Mississippi folklore." It is clear that Faulkner had long been interested in the tall tale, having employed it first in *Mosquitoes*.

Chapter 11. The Wilderness Theme

[1] Random House, 1942.

[2] "Pantaloon in Black," which is an ironical story of white misunderstanding of the terrible excesses of human feeling in a young Negro, a very moving story, falls outside the two strands of subject matter. As an example of the free use Faulkner makes of his subject matter it may be noted that this story is recapitulated briefly in *Requiem for a Nun*.

[3] This was published in the *Saturday Evening Post*, 214 (May 9, 1942), 30–31, the same year the revised version appeared as a part of *Go Down Moses*, but obviously it had been written earlier.

[4] *Spirit of the Times*, 1841.

[5] *Harper's*, 172 (December 1935), 67–77.

Notes

Chapter 12. Sectionalism, and the Detective Story

[1] Random House, 1948.

[2] Random House, 1949.

Chapter 13. The Right to Responsibility

[1] Footnote on the "Second best bed": Lest future bardolaters infer incompatibility to be the reason that Mrs. Faulkner remained behind in Oxford, I feel impelled to put down the actual reason, told to me by a friend of the Faulkner family: she had had her teeth removed and her new dentures were not ready.

[2] Random House, 1950.

[3] Greenville, Mississippi, 1951.

[4] In June 1953 Faulkner gave the commencement address at another of Jill's graduations, this time from Pine Manor Junior College, Wellesley, Mass. (See "Faith or Fear," *Atlantic Monthly*, 192 [August 1953], 53–55.)

[5] Random House, 1951.

Chapter 14. A Concluding View

[1] *Faulkner Studies*, beginning with its Spring 1952 issue, has undertaken to make a survey of the scholarship and criticism devoted to the work of William Faulkner. The magazine is issued quarterly. Formerly published in Denver, its address is now Box 102, University Station, Minneapolis 14, Minn.

A recent article on Faulkner and his family's history is "The Private World of William Faulkner," by Robert Coughlan, in *Life*, September 28 and October 5, 1953.

INDEX

Index

The Tangled Fire of William Faulkner

toris, 8, 9, 88–86; *Soldiers' Pay,* 27–30, 160; *The Sound and the Fury,* 9, 37–45, 84, 160; *These Thirteen,* 66–71, 160; *The Unvanquished,* 8, 11–12, 86, 100–103, 160
Faulkner Studies, 177
Fin de siècle, 16–18
"Fire and the Hearth, The," 126
Folklore, 116–118, 129n
Foster, R. E., 176
Frenchman's Bend, 111–124, 175
Freudian milieu, 70–71, 162

Gant, Miss Zilphia, 70–71
Georgia Scenes, 116, 176
Gide, André, 135
Gilligan, Joe, 27–29
Go Down Moses, 125–134, 161
"Go Down Moses," 126
Goodwin, Lee, 58–59
Goodwin, Ruby, 58–59
Gowrie family, 137–138, 140
Great Gatsby, The, 45, 153
Green Bough, A, 88
Grierson, Miss Emily, 68n, 71
Grimm, Percy, 82
Grove, Lena, 73, 82–83

"Hair," 68
Hamlet, The, 9, 10, 111–124
"Hand upon the Waters," 144
Harris, George W., 123
Hawks, Howard, 56–57
Hemingway, Ernest, 67, 167
Henry V, 175
Hightower, Gail, 78–82, 83
Hines, Euphues, 73, 74
History, southern, Faulkner's approach to, 9–11, 39, 41, 68–69n, 94–98, 100–101, 111–114, 134, 163–164
Hoffman, F. J., 170
Hogganbeck, Boon, 131–132
Holland, Anse, 142–143
Hollywood, 56–57n, 88–89n, 135–136n, 173
"Honor," 89
"Hound, The," 89
Howe, Irving, 23, 175
Hudson, Arthur Palmer, 103, 112–113, 176

Idyll in the Desert, 65–66

Ikkemotube, 69, 126, 172
Imagery, *see* Symbolism
Intruder in the Dust: book, 86, 136–142, 161; film, 150, 151
Isom, fictional character, 13
Isom, Thomas Dudley, 13

Jefferson, mythical town of, 3–15, 137, 139. *See also* Oxford
Johnson, Nunnally, 56–57
Jones, Januarius, 27–28
Jones, Milly, 97
Jones, Wash, 89, 97, 100
Joyce, James, 42
"Justice, A," 69

Knight's Gambit, 142–145
"Knight's Gambit," 145

Lafayette County, 12, 167
"L'Apres Midi d'un Faune," 16
Lewis, Wyndham, 27
Light in August, 72–86
"Lilacs, The," 25
"Lion," 131–132
Longstreet, A. B., 116–117, 176
"Love Song of J. Alfred Prufrock, The," 25–26

McCallum family, 34–35, 114
McCannon, Shreve, 94, 99
McCarron, Hoake, 119
McCaslin family, 11, 69, 112, 125–134
McEachern, Simon, 73–75
Machine, the, 61–64, 89–93, 139
Mahon, Donald, 27
Mallison, Chick, 138–140
Man, modern, in search of belief, *see* Themes
Mannigoe, Nancy, 68, 157–158
Marble Faun, The, 4, 21, 88
Maurier, Mrs., in *Mosquitoes,* 30
Millard, Granny, 101, 173
Miner, Ward, 94
"Mirrors of Chartres Street," in New Orleans *Times Picayune,* 25–26, 169
Miss Zilphia Gant, 70–71, 162
Mississippi, University of, 12, 13, 19, 20, 136
"Mistral," 70
Mitchell, Belle, 34
"Monk," 143

180

Index